NO DOMAIN

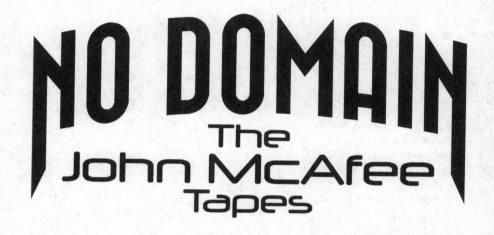

The John McAfee Tapes

MARK EGLINTON

Post Hill Press

A POST HILL PRESS BOOK
ISBN: 978-1-64293-953-8
ISBN (eBook): 978-1-64293-954-5

No Domain:
The John McAfee Tapes

Cover photo by Philippe Fatoux
Cover art by Cody Corcoran

All people, locations, events, and situations are portrayed to the best of the author's memory. While all of the events described are true, many names and identifying details have been changed to protect the privacy of the people involved.

Post Hill Press
New York • Nashville
posthillpress.com

Published in the United States of America
1 2 3 4 5 6 7 8 9 10

CONTENTS

PROLOGUE

In October of 2019, I direct messaged John McAfee on Twitter after we made contact about the possibility of working together on an autobiography. To continue the dialogue was a no-brainer.

John McAfee was the embodiment of many of the reasons that led me to become a co-writer in the first place. I saw him as a true white whale.

At first glance, McAfee's life had been as colorful as any writer could hope for. Indeed, much of what is rumored to have happened in his seventy-four years is maybe too colorful to publish at all: murder accusations, rumors of involvement with all kinds of drugs and harems of young women, the suggestion that he might have fathered a few dozen children.

All of this was plentiful online, as were rumors about run-ins with the IRS, with whom he'd apparently refused to file a tax return for over a decade. And there was plenty more besides, beginning with a relatively normal early life (by McAfee standards at least) whereby, having breezed into the computer programming world as some kind of math prodigy, he founded the world's first antivirus software company in 1987 and then walked away with an estimated $100 million when he benefitted from the stock market flotation of the company seven years later.

Beyond that, there's the libertarian stance that gives him a strange and rather ironic affinity, in his capacity as a former multi-millionaire executive, with the downtrodden in society, a group to which, by his own admission, he has constantly been drawn throughout his life.

Indeed, McAfee's general distrust of authority and the elite, in combination with an attachment to the disenfranchised, has led him to run, on two occasions, in US presidential elections as a semi-legitimate Libertarian Party candidate.

Perhaps more significant to me was the fact that there is an undeniable air of raw danger and mystery surrounding the man that's hard to resist. What writer could refuse the prospect of a subject who had been alternately on the run and in hiding, wearing disguises, toting shotguns bare-chested, faking heart attacks to avoid arrest, all over the world, for the last few years?

I certainly couldn't.

I know that to the outsider, many of John McAfee's behaviors appear outlandishly impulsive and irresponsible. But however much he can come across a little unhinged, the reality is that for a far greater proportion of the time, he's a balanced, thoughtful man, a Delphic Oracle figure, dispensing random soundbites simply to be interpreted in whatever way the listener chooses, but beneath it all lies a grasp of subjects that are incredibly relevant to the world today. To me, this dichotomy is what makes a guy like John McAfee matter in a world turned upside down amid a worldwide pandemic.

To that end, the scope of subject matter for a life-spanning memoir was never in doubt. There was enough in the King of Misinformation's life for three books. And while I'd never written any fiction, it was immediately clear that any book where McAfee was involved was going to flirt with the blurred boundaries between reality and fiction to the extent that I'd accepted I'd probably be in a perpetual state of being willingly gaslit.

I also knew that, above anything else, I needed the man to engage completely (or as completely as he'd lead me to believe he was engaging) for the collaboration to go anywhere. After all, for someone as wary as he'd become in recent years, nothing was ever certain.

True to form, for a few days, nothing happened. After a week of silence, I followed up with a polite request for an email address to which I could forward a business proposition. An email address immediately appeared. I used it, laying out a one-page bullet-pointed plan designed to both appeal to his ego and to make the process sound like it would be easy.

"Will it cost me anything?" came the reply.

"No," I said. "But one condition I do have is that I need to see your face on a video call before we even start."

We exchanged Skype IDs, and I told him that I'd be available to talk face-to-face later that evening.

Only a few minutes later (not "that evening" as I'd suggested), while I was driving between Edinburgh and my hometown, a ninety-minute trip mostly on motorway, the Skype app on my phone lit up. I looked at my wife, who could also see the screen in the center console between us that said, "McAfee Nomad."

"You've got to answer it," she said.

She was right. I had to. We both knew he might never call again. I veered off the motorway exit, pulled into a gas station, and picked up the call. John McAfee, face framed with dark, wraparound sunglasses, stared back.

I had no idea where he was, I never did, and he didn't ever care to ask where I was. None of that mattered. Nevertheless, over the next few days and weeks, we gradually pieced together a framework for a book that would aim to demystify the man for the first time. Writers had started and either been fired or had given up, he told me. Via my own research, I'd read that one such writer, the late former cocaine trafficker George "Boston George" Jung, was rumored to have been commissioned to write an official biography. At no point was that relationship ever discussed.

"These people just weren't open-minded enough to accept some of the things I was telling them," he said in blanket reference to all previous writing relationships. I wondered whether one day he'd be saying the same about me.

Then, as if to convince me of his story's worth, he proudly regaled me with quick-fire tales, like how he messed with the heads of various journalists who sought him out while he was holed up in Belize in 2012. On one occasion, he pointed a loaded revolver at his own forehead and pulled the trigger.

"That fucker was naïve. I tricked him," McAfee told me, laughing a little more maniacally than I was comfortable with. "And he totally lost his shit and left."

Then there was the one about the *Financial Times* journalist who came out to Belize and found himself blindfolded and driven around the city before being thrust into hiding above a Chinese supermarket in Belize City with an assorted cast of McAfee's crew of ex-cons.

"He took one look around the room after five minutes and said, 'I totally underestimated what I was getting into. I'm leaving,'" he explained, with pride, all while I sat in my car at a petrol station.

I knew that McAfee was testing me on a couple of levels. First, he wanted to make it clear that we would speak when *he* wanted to—and that I'd answer whenever he called. On this occasion, I did, because I had to. As time passed, I would create boundaries. Second, he wanted to see if I was shocked or even whether I sought to ingratiate myself to him by finding his stories amusing. Knowing he'd see either as a sign of weakness, I gave him neither response. I just stared back, wondering what the hell I was getting myself into.

And yet, given that I was already faced with sound reasons to run a mile from the project, you'd be entitled to wonder why I continued. The truth is that I was sufficiently allured by the McAfee mystique to keep going. Not just that, I was titillated enough to do it all with absolutely no written or verbal collaboration agreement. What's the point when you're dealing with a man who's in hiding, on the run from the CIA, with more than a hundred lawsuits active against him? I was hardly going to go after him. We both knew that. In some ways, it made for a simpler arrangement—but not one that any agent/legal adviser would countenance for a second. We also never discussed money other than his initial query—another absolute no-no that I willingly ignored.

Instead, like McAfee had done his entire life, I just rolled the dice. And over the following days, we proceeded with our plan to write this book that he told me he has always threatened to write in response to constant demands from his million-strong army of Twitter followers.

"I never found the right person. But I sensed right away you were the guy," he said.

Buoyed by this dubious endorsement, I descended into McAfee's world headfirst. So complex and delicate was the working relationship initially that the idea of a finished book seemed always like a comedic notion—just a barely flickering light in the distance.

We talked for hours, days, over many weeks. McAfee alternated between being emotional and overwrought and polite and courteous. Sometimes, he was drinking; other times, he appeared high, agitated, and literally looking over his shoulder as we talked. Whenever his wife, a former prostitute he met when he returned to the US from Belize in 2013, brought him a cup of coffee, he made a point of making her drink some first.

"You see, Janice has tried to kill me several times," he told me. "I'd like to think I can trust her, but can we ever trust anyone?"

Hmmm, I thought.

Regardless, John McAfee promised to tell me his life story in many, many layers. This was to be his truth, he said. How his abusive father had shot himself in the head with a shotgun in the family bathroom when he was just a teenage boy. How, through his affinity with mathematics, he found a way to simultaneously be an indispensable polymath genius and also ride roughshod over almost every major company that hired him in his thirties—showing up as infrequently as possible to whatever office he'd been hired to run. How, after a life-changing hallucinogenic drug trip, he drove three hundred miles with a view to killing his first wife and daughter, having been told by voices to do so. (A preacher he met along the way talked him out of it.) How, having received an astronomical sum when McAfee Associates was floated on the stock exchange, he embarked on a spree of building outlandish houses all over the world, sometimes at the cost of many millions of dollars each, only to set foot in just a handful of them. How, after giving away all of his possessions from the driveway of his remote Colorado mansion, he moved to Belize for a quiet life and instead became a pariah in the eyes of government militia, from whom he'd ultimately flee the country with the help of a Guatemalan government official, having been framed, he said, for the murder of his American neighbor.

On and on it went. There was so much to process.

How could one life possibly have so many dimensions?

How could it all be true?

How the hell was this man still alive?

These were just a few of the questions I asked myself on an hourly basis, but at the same time, I found myself growing fond of the man in a way that I hadn't foreseen. Even I couldn't deny that, despite his faults—and he admitted to many—there was an admirable authenticity and purity to the way McAfee had lived that I had to respect, even if I didn't relate to or approve of most of what he said and had done.

"It's important to say that, when you tell my story, you, as the first person to understand this complex narrative, make an important connection between the press and the chaos I find myself in. It's an entire ball of wax, a tornado that I have been swept up in. I had no control other than trying to dodge all the debris that has been swept up also. So, that being said, I can't overstate the connection between the press and my life. And in some cases, the press has been driven more by people who have personal dislikes for me than by people who are objective and just want to write an article containing the facts about what's actually happening. All of that has impacted my life more than anyone can ever understand," he was at pains to tell me.

Then, with the working relationship seemingly unshakeable, things got really fucking weird.

We had secured an initial agreement for a book deal with a publisher whose values aligned with his guerrilla outlook. But as we reached the brink of signing, a hitch surfaced.

"Payment in cryptocurrency only," the Skype instant message said. "I will only accept DAI direct from the publisher."

For the uninitiated, DAI is a crypto-backed stablecoin that's loosely linked ("pegged") in value to the US dollar. It is a form of decentralized finance, with the aim of decentralization being to reimagine existing financial systems, making them more transparent, interlinked, permissionless, and "trustless." While its supply is based entirely on demand, the reality is that few outside the cryptocurrency world will have even heard of DAI, much less know how to acquire it or use it. I was similarly clueless—the publisher's finance department, I suspected, would be equally so.

"Isn't there a way around this with me receiving payment or something?" I asked him.

I was scrambling not to lose the deal—and didn't even really know how such a suggestion could work.

"Payments will go on indefinitely. You might die...." McAfee countered.

Reeling from that suggestion, I suspected right away that all of this was a potential deal-breaker. Publishers don't pay in cryptocurrency, much less this obscure variant he was insisting on. I protested, saying that had I known of this condition at the outset, I wouldn't have started the process in the first place.

"Publishing seems to be the only business in the entire world that cannot use cryptocurrency. Fuck them," was his terse sign-off to me one evening.

This assertion was patently incorrect, though. As traditionally "establishment" as publishing is, it is by no means the only industry sector that's not yet conversant with the crypto world. Even I knew that McAfee's idea of utopia—a cashless society where traditional financial institutions are rendered impotent—was at the very least some years away.

"I will ask the question," I told him. "But if they can't do it, are you saying that this book is dead in the water?"

"I will not, under any fucking circumstances, at any fucking time, for any fucking reason, budge from this position. I am sorry, my friend. Do not push me in this, or you and I are finished," he replied.

Of course, satisfying this request was impossible. Not only that, the absence of an actual mailing address via which a publisher could reliably contract with him was another issue that was simply insurmountable. There were just too many red flags.

So I didn't push him. I walked away instead. He was right: we were finished as a collaborative team. But the idea of a book wasn't, at least not for me. With good faith, he and I had set out in October 2019 to write a particular book. This, however, isn't that book. This is something else entirely.

Ironically, during the process of talking to McAfee, I kept having this nagging doubt as to whether his story could best be told exclusively from his standpoint anyway. Given the nature of some of the events, not to mention the machinations of the man's personality quirks, where you must constantly be on guard against being tricked, I continually wrestled with whether he just didn't have enough perspective on *himself* to make a true, conventional autobiography credible. Someone had to hold him to task as much as is possible. We even discussed whether he could simply authorize me to tell his story.

As it turned out, his departure from the project made any decision about the style of the book much easier. I felt that a book written in the form of a conversation would allow a slightly more objective view on all of these happenings. Yes, McAfee's exact words could and would be used, as they would have been in a straight memoir format. Better still, for McAfee himself not to be directly involved served to circumnavigate some of the obvious legal and financial issues that might arise from publishing a book by a mercurial man, but also one who is now in jail with a reputed 172 lawsuits out against him.

Either way, the further irony is that, in pulling out at the eleventh hour, John McAfee might just have facilitated the most viable book about himself and his extraordinary life. There's even a small part of me that wonders, knowing him as I do, whether this was the way he always intended it. I'll probably never know. Either way, here we are. Welcome to the confusing world of John McAfee.

ONE

THE CHASE / THE CIA

In 2012, it was difficult to avoid seeing images of John McAfee online. By his own design and with the help/hindrance of journalists from *VICE* (they accidentally revealed his position via the location data published in an image posted on their website), he'd made his escape from Belize via Guatemala big news.

But the McAfee we were seeing in 2012 was visually worlds away from the man we thought we knew, that being the smooth-talking, vaguely hippy-looking bon-viveur with sun-kissed highlights and a disarming smile, as opposed to the facially drawn, wide-eyed, and dyed-hair version.

McAfee's flight from Belize wasn't just a reaction to a state of deepening friction between him and the Belizean government that had been steadily going bad; it was the culmination of a lifetime of behaviors, all of which were informed in some way by the day his abusive, alcoholic father committed suicide while John was an impressionable, rebellious teenager living in Salem, Virginia.

McAfee's relationship with his father had been fractious, to say the least. And because young John often bore the brunt of his father's drunken alter ego, a skewed view of authority developed that would last a lifetime.

Two questions had burned in me from the moment I first learned that John McAfee was on the lam again in 2019. Where was he? And who or what was he running from?

Let's backtrack for a second.

Ever since returning to the US from Belize via Guatemala in 2012, McAfee claims to have been chased around the US by a disparate cast of bad guys ranging from US-based heavies contracted by the Belizean government to members of the infamous Sinaloa Cartel in Mexico.

He also claimed that his wife, Janice, a prostitute he met in Miami on his first day back in the US, was in cahoots with at least one of the above and, for several years, via her former pimp, in on the plot to kill or apprehend him.

From Miami to Portland to Tennessee and, finally, to North Carolina, McAfee ran for several years, with Janice in tow. At one point, having had his cover blown, he hid in an underground parking garage in Portland while his pursuers circled above. On another occasion, a sniper in a field beside a highway in Arizona shot at his pickup truck.

What ultimately forced the issue, he says, was when his entourage caught wind of the fact that a grand jury had been convened in Tennessee, indicting him and four members of his 2020 presidential campaign team on tax-related charges. There was also the small matter of a wrongful death lawsuit relating to his former neighbor in Belize, Gregory Faull, which the Circuit Court in Orlando, Florida, was simply refusing to dismiss.

On paper, John McAfee definitely had a number of reasons to flee the US in early 2019. And he did just that, in typically ostentatious style. He bought a yacht—*The Great Mystery*—and instead of slipping out to sea under cover of darkness like any other fugitive, he documented the cash sale in an online video post before taking off into international waters, first docking in the Bahamas, then in Havana, Cuba, and, finally, in the Dominican Republic, where he was arrested in Puerto Plata on what he claimed was a trumped-up firearms-related charge.

According to him, the CIA, having first attempted to apprehend him in Nassau, had later flown down to the Dominican Republic to facilitate his deportation back to the US. Instead, after faking a stroke to buy time after having spent four days in jail, from where he posted pictures of himself smiling with fellow inmates online, he and Janice were indeed deported, not to the US, but to the UK, his country of birth.

That's the abridged version of the reasons John McAfee left the US. More on that later. For now, though, having got to London, the dual UK/US citizen McAfee went completely dark. No tweets, nothing by way of blog entries—just silence. He had disappeared, which wasn't something he was accustomed to doing, given how partial he has always been to self-promotion.

Now, in October 2019, here he was, in front of me on a computer screen from who knows where.

Getting him there had been little fraught, it should be said. His mood, transmitted clearly via his emails, swung between monosyllabic and distant. The formatting was always the same. He never addressed me directly by name, and he never signed off with his.

In between, the text was comprised of single sentences with an exaggerated amount of space between. These statements, I assumed, were presented in a way that they'd have maximum impact. "Send me two or three links to your work if you ever want me to respond again," was one of these statements in our earliest exchanges. Eventually, after a bit of email brinksmanship on both sides, we got there.

Visually, even on a video call, John McAfee cuts a confusing figure. For a man of seventy-four years old with many drug and alcohol miles on the clock dating back to his early, pre-McAfee Associates days, he looks surprisingly well: goatee, broad, healthy smile, tattoo on the chest that reads "Privacy, Freedom, Technology," and hair that appeared to permanently have some kind of electric charge pulsing through it.

On our many calls, he often wore sunglasses, regardless of the time of day, and when he didn't, his eyes had a look that I hadn't exactly bargained for. These weren't the eyes of a madman—not at all. They had instead a potential for great kindness and deep empathy—offset by the knowing glint of a seasoned liver of life. It was, however, his voice that stood out.

Although he was British, born to an English mother and US airman father, and grew up in rural Virginia, his speaking voice, which often took on a kind of breathy, quivering, thespian grandiosity, could have been from anywhere in the US. With it, he often attempted to filibuster my direct questions, and in the beginning, I let him, simply because of the novelty value of listening to him. Initially, I enjoyed hearing him eulogize.

Pretty soon, though, entertainment had to give way to the actual purpose of our talks: his life story. And to that end, I felt this need to ground myself in some kind of reality with the McAfee myth. To do so, the first thing I had to establish was whether anyone was actually looking for him at all. And if they were, from whom was he running?

The way I saw it, if US authorities could pull Saddam Hussein from a hole in the ground in Iraq and track Bin Laden down to some nondescript house in Pakistan, *surely* they could find and apprehend John McAfee if they really wanted to? Nothing about his situation added up.

"At some point, you'll need to come and visit us," he told me on one of our first Skype calls, "but I can't tell you where I am. You'll go to an airport, someone will meet you with a ticket, and you will board a plane. That's all I can tell you."

For obvious reasons, this was, at best, a confusing proposal and absolutely the stuff of spy movies. Although I agreed at the time because I'd have done anything to get the material, it was the only occasion during my several months talking to McAfee that the idea of meeting in person was ever mentioned.

Whether it was a trust thing and our daily face-to-face Skype calls served to ease that concern for him, I don't know, but the idea of meeting in person just went away, as many things did during our long and often tangential conversations. Nevertheless, I pressed him on the existence and nature of the imminent threat without ever asking directly where he was. I needed the background to this in-hiding status.

••••••••••●•••••••••

ME: I understand that you're in hiding. But for me to understand you and why you are in the situation you are in, I also need to comprehend why the CIA specifically wants to bring you in at all?

John McAfee: Let's just say that my current relationship with the CIA really isn't very good. They don't want to kill me per se, but I am undoubtedly a nuisance to them—and for a couple of reasons. Firstly, when I was in Cuba, I was in communication with their government about creating a cryptocurrency system that would allow them to avoid US sanctions. There were probably only a handful of people in the world at that time that knew enough about blockchain technology to be able to do that, but I was one of them. This was all over in the newspapers in Cuba and the internet, and that doesn't exactly make any friends in the US, does it?

And then there's the issue of tax, for which I haven't filed returns for ten years. For eight years, the IRS just turned a blind eye to that—just like that, they've let many people off filing tax returns and even paying tax. It was only when I went out there and started talking on national stages, at conferences, saying things like, "I think tax is illegal. Therefore, if you don't want to pay, here's how you do it," that I became a problem to them. That's why they convened a grand jury to indict Janice and me, and that's why we left the country.

ME: But where does the CIA fit into this? Why do they even care?

John McAfee: Once a person leaves America, there is only one organization that can help America bring that person back. And that's the CIA. The FBI can't operate outside America. The military cannot, according to any international law, go around collecting people who don't pay their taxes. That job is left to the CIA, and that's where the dichotomy arises in my instance in the sense that some of the people in the CIA are warning me of impending events before they happen. The youngest of these friends of mine is in his sixties. These people are on their way out. But I take action when they tell me things nevertheless.

Meanwhile, other divisions within the organization have no choice but to cooperate when someone like the IRS or someone else at a low level in the executive branch says, "McAfee is a problem. This guy is outside the country now. He's damaging us politically. Can you help us out?" And, of course, the CIA will.

ME: On a practical level, how do they bring someone like you in?

John McAfee: Sometimes they'll outright kidnap people. But most of the time, they do what they've been doing to me, and they'll lean on the governments of other countries to force someone to return to the US. And the CIA can do that because they're embedded in *every* government, spreading money out like butter on bread wherever they go.

The State Department is just a branch of the CIA. All US embassies worldwide have staff working for the CIA. Why? Because that's how they get the CIA into the country. They get given the black passport, and that's a "get out of jail" card no matter what they do. They could walk into St. Peter's Square, grab a child, and chew off its left arm. Nobody could touch them.

The Dominican Republic in 2019 was case in point of how the CIA is embedded in embassies everywhere. It was a perfect setup. After we'd been told by our previous port of call, Cuba, that we had to leave the country because the US government had requested that we be returned to America, Cuba said that they hadn't replied to that request and probably wouldn't for a few days.

So it was a case of "Mr. McAfee, we'd like you to leave Cuba within seventy-two hours." We leave, of course, and when we arrive in the Dominican Republic a day and a half later, armed soldiers are lining the dock, surrounding the boat.

They refused to let us talk to customs or immigration; meanwhile, we have our various weapons laid out on the table, un-chambered, unloaded, just as normal. Regardless, we were arrested and charged with bringing illegal weapons into the country without declaration. Please, God, how could I declare them if I couldn't talk to customs?

I knew immediately that this was the CIA, and I also knew that they intended this operation to be so swift that there would be no time for any legal recourse. It was totally illegal and unconstitutional, and had they succeeded, that wouldn't have mattered. I'd have been in jail in the US and never heard from again. However, I'd been through this kind of shit before.

ME: You knew what was about to happen?

John McAfee: Of course! I knew exactly what was going down. Meanwhile, as we were being driven around, I even identified the CIA agent. When I first spoke with him I said, "What did you say your name was, sir?"

"Jim" he said.

"And your surname?" I continued.

"It is just…Jim."

"Do you have a business card then, Jim?" I said.

"No," he told me.

He may have been presenting himself as some lowly embassy official, but I saw through that mirage. He fitted the profile: ex-military, multiple languages. And as I was looking at him, he was also looking at me in the same fucking way. He knew that I knew.

ME: Are you saying that you recognized each other for what you were?

John McAfee: Exactly. There was a certain mutual understanding of what the relationship was. He even made a joke about it on the second day: "Why didn't you just call us at the embassy immediately when this happened?" he said, with a knowing look in his eye.

As if, I thought to myself.

Initially, they didn't even let lawyers talk to us. But, as they were transferring us from one police station to another, these two opportunist, ambulance-chasing lawyers grabbed me in the hallway and got me to sign something. They were just doing what lawyers do: looking for potential clients. With lawyer representation, the world changes. Meanwhile, we were moved to another part of the island and thrown in this awful outdoor jail for the night.

ME: Did you think there was a way out at that point?

John McAfee: There is always a way out, my friend. The next morning, immigration officers came to us and said: "Mr. McAfee, we're not going to punish you for what you have done. Instead, we're just going to send you back to America."

"I'd prefer to go to England," I replied, pulling out my British passport. "Sorry, sir, you have to go back to America," came the response.

Meanwhile, they had Janice ready to be put on a flight, so I asked my lawyer to file a brief requesting I have my say in court. And thank God, it wasn't the weekend, or else we'd have been so fucked. "How long will it take to file the brief?' I asked the lawyers. "It'll take two hours," they told me.

ME: Sounds like you were backed into a corner.

John McAfee: I absolutely was. So I faked a stroke, got taken to the hospital, and bought the time we needed. And ever since then, their pursuit of me continues, whereby they try to find ways to pick me up that don't involve sending a SEAL team in the middle of the night, and instead one that usually involves manufacturing crimes to get me into custody in America because once you're in custody, you're lost forever, my friend.

So my only recourse is to keep running from country to country, simply because it takes them time to set something up. I can't let them know where I am, and I know how to do that, and have been doing it successfully for six months.

McAfee's explanation of his current situation in hiding seemed perfectly plausible. But I didn't quite know whether it was plausible because it was true or because I was simply talking to a master manipulator. I mean, if he could fake a stroke to buy time from the CIA in the Dominican Republic, it stood to reason that he could probably fool me with his fanciful stories of evading nonexistent pursuers. What struck me most was how calm he seemed about it all.

Regardless, there was no doubt that the man did have a direct relationship with the CIA, which dated back to his own work with the organization, which had begun in the mid-1980s while he was working on top-secret government contracts after having been identified for the role while he was an employee working for Lockheed Martin, the military contractor.

John McAfee: I had to go through an outrageous daylong interrogation process to get my clearance to work on that black program. "Have you ever taken drugs?" "Yes." "What drugs?" "Pretty much everything." "Did you ever sell drugs?" "Yes." "What kind?" "All." "Have you ever cheated on your wife?" "Yes." "How many times?" "As often as I could."

That's pretty much how I responded to these questions, and I did so because they already knew the answers. You cannot lie to these people. In the two to three weeks between when they contact you for an interview and you show up, they are finding everything about you. Who you are; the first time you masturbated. There is nothing they won't know. So you've got to answer truthfully.

After the interview, I went back to my job at Lockheed, thinking there was no fucking chance I'd get clearance. I had a female boss, and she kept saying, "Just relax." Two and a half weeks later, I got my clearance. This is just conjecture on my part, but I think I got it because it was pretty clear that nobody was going to be able to blackmail me given how direct and matter-of-fact I was about all my answers. Getting that security clearance was the biggest shock to me, having openly declared a life of total debauchery.

Nevertheless, I worked on one black program for a year and a half, and I only finished working on it just a month before I started McAfee in 1987. I was chosen for two reasons. First, I was working for Lockheed Martin at the time—the largest military contractor. In those days, the government always selected people from military contractor backgrounds. Second, they wanted me because I had a unique software talent. By that point, I'd already developed the first-ever voice recognition software and sold it.

The shit I was working on there was used three years later. But it wasn't officially announced for a further twenty-two years. Twenty-two fucking years! That's how far ahead they worked back then. It's probably fifty years nowadays.

ME: What exactly is a CIA black program? Where did all of this start?

John McAfee: The atomic bomb, for example, was built inside a black program, meaning that nobody could know about it, including the president. Everyone in a black program must be cleared. Everyone is warned of the dire consequences that await him or her should any information ever be divulged. Those consequences are execution.

ME: Who is overseeing this and issuing these directives?

John McAfee: You have asked the question of all questions, my friend. In our country, we have presidents, Congress, senators, and so on. We elect these officials, we give them certain powers, and we believe that this is the American government. But let me tell you the truth of this: behind the American government is the Central Intelligence Agency. The CIA is a necessary evil that we didn't elect, but who now control the flow of information all over the world. The organization was formed in the middle of the last century and was first warned about by President Eisenhower, who once said something to the effect of, "Beware of the

CIA and of the military-industrial complex." He said this because he saw where the CIA was headed.

ME: What is their actual role?

John McAfee: The power of the CIA is based on a tiny principle. That principle is simply called "need to know." And this is where the madness begins. These people in the CIA never quit. Unless they get whacked, they are there for life. And they are patriots. The CIA views presidents and administrations as transients: in for four or eight years, and then someone else comes along. Meanwhile, the CIA is a constant.

So, when a new president comes into office and gets the same security clearance as I had, he too is subject to "need to know." If he says, "So, do we have evidence of aliens?" he would be told, "Mr. President, sir, I regret to say that you do not have 'need to know.'" This is where the CIA became too powerful. They have the ultimate power of veto and, as such, are answerable to nobody.

The other side of the argument is that "need to know" is logical. Because if everyone was told everything they thought they deserved to know, pretty soon, there would be no secrets. So, mathematically speaking, the CIA had to happen. They were created to be the owners of information. In the 1950s and 1960s, that's one thing. The moderately abusive power they had then was bad enough, even though, at the time, they could do much less with it. But can you imagine how much power they acquired when the world approached the information age? Suddenly, computers and the internet came along. At that point, not only does the CIA know everything, but they also have the power *not* to tell you anything—whoever the fuck you are.

ME: Is it the CIA's place to be economical with the truth?

John McAfee: With very few exceptions, the CIA will tell the president and Congress the truth. However, it's more a question of what truth the CIA wants to tell and when.

Let's say the issue was gun control back before the era of information. If it was in the CIA's interest for people to be able to carry guns, they would have the power to control the information in the sense that, if 100,000 people died one year because of guns and 50 people were saved because of them, they could choose only to talk about the little grandma in North Dakota who shot the intruder who was trying to break into her home, and not the 100,000 others who were shot in all kinds of other hideous circumstances.

And then, when you extend that information set into all other areas—finance, business, international relations, politics, history, political alliances, etc. —they have total command over more information than any one president could ever learn. There are very few exceptions when the CIA doesn't have the upper hand.

ME: What exceptions?

John McAfee: As Iraq was gaining power in the Middle East, the CIA became unsettled because what was happening went against whatever it was that they wanted to achieve in that region at the time, in relation to God knows what. After one failed attempt to assassinate Saddam Hussein in the '90s, they realized that assassinating him would only make things worse. He had sons, brothers, relatives, and they knew they couldn't whack them all. Fast-forward to 2003, and at that point, the CIA knew that the only way they could protect their interests in the region was to bomb Iraq.

The CIA basically went to President Bush and said words to the effect of, "Mr. President, sir, please sit down because we have extraordinarily bad news. We know that Iraq has missiles capable of reaching the UK, our closest ally. But we now know with 100 percent certainty that Iraq has nuclear weapons."

The CIA knew they didn't have these weapons. The general public and every other country in the world knew too. But the CIA talked seriously enough to President Bush that they knew he would have to act. He was always going to declare war. It's not common for them to lie to presidents, but with Iraq, they had no other way of protecting their own interests. They had to construct a case, and they did. It was a fucking tragedy.

ME: How do you know all of this? Are you getting this information directly from CIA friends?

John McAfee: I rarely discuss this kind of stuff, but lately, I have had to because people just think I'm a fucking conspiracy theorist. But I know people in the CIA. One of them still emails me every other day, and we physically talk once a week.

This individual was a former station manager. He is now as retired as anyone ever is from the organization. The CIA, from a day-to-day perspective, does retire people theoretically—they have to when operatives reach sixty-five—but they never really retire. They continue to get the same paycheck from a secret corporation, funded by God knows what, rather than from the government. Same amount, same benefits, just a different entity doing the actual paying. So, my friend, while technically "retired," is still there. And while he is, he talks to me and informs me of anything that is pertinent to my situation.

Beyond that, the CIA was one of my first customers when I started McAfee Associates because I was basically the only computer security company in existence back in 1987. I know as much, if not more, than any politician about what goes on inside these covert agencies like the CIA. And, for that reason, I know exactly why they are looking for me, and, over the years, I've learned how to make quick moves when I'm in a corner. I'll keep doing that as long as I'm alive.

ME: You've escaped from a few tight corners over the years. Where does this innate ability to understand the dynamics of a situation come from? Is it a natural ability or something you learned?

John McAfee: Escaping tricky situations almost always comes down to timing. *Timing*. On the occasions in my life when I dealt drugs—for example, when I was traveling around Mexico with my girlfriend in the late '70s—I learned this. It was never anything serious; I was just earning a few extra bucks. Nevertheless, people would come to me all the time and ask me, "What happens when you finally get caught?" I always told them the same thing: "You better have it settled within the first twenty seconds of the encounter, or else it's all over."

Generally speaking, in these early moments, there's usually only one guy or maybe two. It's at that point that you've got to make a move of some kind—take the one guy aside, whisper something in his ear or offer cash. Do whatever, and do it quickly.

I know of one instance of this couple who got caught dealing drugs and had no money to bribe anyone. The guy said, "Would you like my girl for a while, instead?" They made a move, a move not to be judged by the way, because these were the days when they would have gone to jail for thirty years in Mexico for dealing drugs.

I have no idea where I learned this ability to do something quickly. In fact, at times, I think it's more about perceiving the absolute reality of your situation. I've been in enough situations in my life to understand these realities.

And in the Dominican Republic in 2019, when the soldiers came onto my boat before I'd even gone through customs or officially entered the country, I recognized the reality again. I'd been all over the world on boats and in every port that has access to the sea. I knew how the system works. When they came aboard without even letting me talk to customs, I thought, *Fuck me. Thank you, Cuba*. It took me four days to get from Cuba to the Dominican Republic. Within thirty seconds of my boat leaving Cuba, the CIA probably knew exactly where I was going.

From there, I just reacted to my reality as it unfolded. I had no idea I was going to have to fake illness and go to the hospital to buy time. These things just happened, even after I was assigned lawyers. They played their hand; then I played mine. I just counted on myself to understand the realities as they presented themselves. And when I did, and it reached a point where I clearly understood what everyone was trying to achieve, I said to myself, "I can deal with this shit," and that's when I took action and faked a stroke. Over time, I have learned to read people, and dealing with my dad when I was growing up in Salem, Virginia, was where I learned.

TWO

SWEET VIRGINIA

I'd been talking to McAfee for two weeks, with an hour-long call every three days or so. Initially, we started formally: "Send Janice an email to book a call into my schedule, and we'll go from there," he told me.

It became apparent that there was no schedule. He wasn't doing anything else as far as I could see. Wherever he was in the world (I never asked, but based on time zone/daylight, I'm guessing it was somewhere in central Europe), he wasn't exactly operating on standard business hours.

Often when I spoke to him, he had either just gotten up or was drinking. Sometimes, he had just gotten up *and* was drinking. Other times, he was still in bed.

It was all a bit disorganized, and there always seemed to be people building in the background of wherever it was that he was living—drilling, hammering, contractors erecting what looked like partition walls. People came and went, some speaking very little English. One was introduced to me on Skype as he walked past with an industrial nail gun. He waved; I gave him the thumbs up. Junior was his name.

From there, we abandoned the formal arranging through Janice and just sent each other messages on Skype instant messenger instead. To the best of my knowledge, McAfee never used a cell phone for regular phone calls, nor did he use any of the standard messaging apps to communicate.

For whatever reason, Skype was the only way he'd willingly engage. That is, until he stopped.

At one point before the third week of calls, McAfee disappeared altogether. Although we had a firm time for a scheduled call, he didn't pick the call up when I rang. When I instant messaged to ask if he needed to reschedule, the message was "read," but no response came back. I went back to Janice with a polite request for another date, and there was no response to that email either.

Part of me thought he might have been captured; a bigger part of me felt sure I would have heard about that online. I just left it for a few days. I could see he was active; Skype showed his status as "online" at various times.

Paranoid, I went through everything we'd discussed to that point in my head and wondered if there was anything he'd told me that he might have wished he hadn't. I couldn't think of anything. I knew he was edgy about discussing some of the events that took place in Belize. We'd touched on that era but had hardly got into it in any depth yet. In any case, at the outset, he'd told me he had nothing to hide on that front anyway.

I then wondered if it was our business arrangement, which was loose, to put it mildly, that was putting him off. All we'd agreed was that, in the event of a publishing deal, we'd split the proceeds and figure out the exact percentages when we knew what we were dividing. We were both pretty relaxed about that side of it all, I thought.

On one hand, McAfee's disappearance was a bit strange because he'd been readily engaging and seemed enthusiastic—borderline excited—to get through as much material as we could. On another, it was probably what I expected. It was John McAfee, after all. What did I expect?

And then, out of nowhere, after a week of no contact, he reappeared as if nothing had happened, although, to his credit, he did apologize for not making the initial call and arranged another for the following day. In the interim, an email arrived which contained the following provisional foreword, written by him, along with a note that explained that he wanted all of the book proceeds to go to the person named (or rather, not named) in the below:

> *"I have been urged for years by my friends to put my life down on paper. It seemed like a step back from newer means of laying out a life, and I always sidestepped the suggestion.*
>
> *I am lazy by nature and would not attempt a project such as writing my autobiography in the absence of duress. That duress arrived when Janice and I went into hiding after our arrest in the Dominican Republic. The man that stepped up and offered assistance gave us food, shelter, and the promise of security.*
>
> *Having temporarily exhausted our resources, my offer of repayment was to spend the time, so freely provided by my host, writing my autobiography and giving full rights to the book and to all proceeds thereof to my host. Once I have an obligation, I do carry it out, and my host fulfilled his end of the promise as well.*
>
> *Janice and I are now free to move, with restrictions, about the world. His many months of shelter saved our lives, and this book is dedicated to him, though he must remain nameless."*

Obviously, this email, and the suggestion within it that all the book proceeds would be going to some anonymous person, was a little unsettling. I called him on Skype for an explanation. "Oh, there's no issue," McAfee said. "Don't worry about the business side of things. I'll take care of that."

"I understand," I said. "But I need to know exactly where I stand before we go much further."

"How about if you take 35 percent of all revenues and I take 65 percent?" he said.

"And you pay your guy from your share, not off the top, right?" I asked.

"Yes," McAfee replied.

"That's very generous, thanks," I said.

Thereafter, neither the foreword nor the mystery beneficiary was ever mentioned again. But at least he and I were back on track with the conversations.

•••••••••●•••••••••

ME: We finished last time with you saying that your relationship with your dad taught you a lot about people. Why was that?

John McAfee: OK, yes, that's right. I learned to read people because of my dad—not that he knew how to read people himself at all. He was an alcoholic and not the nicest of people. He worked as a road surveyor by day, and he drank at night. And when he became unhappy with any situation in his immediate environment, which was often, he'd simply lash out at the closest thing that was able to feel something, and that was usually me.

But I wasn't stupid. I adapted. I became extraordinarily *attentive* to him, not just to his moods themselves, but also to the subtle position of his hands before a bad mood even came on, or the way he might look or how he smiled or didn't smile at a certain moment. The reason for that study was that when a mood came on, it was too late. I learned to pre-empt, and this was done entirely from a place of self-preservation.

Of course, these moods of his could be joyful as much as they could be angry. Either way, I had to learn to recognize the signs and behave accordingly. When he was drinking and happy, well, fuck me, I could have burned the house down, and that would have been fine with him. But when he was angry, I knew I had to be on my best fucking behavior; otherwise, he'd lash out. I learned all this because I wanted to do nothing that would ever push that motherfucker over the edge.

ME: Did your dad physically beat you?

John McAfee: Every kid got the belt when I was a kid. Please, God. If you think there's a single man of my age who was not whipped with a belt more times than he can count, then you are delusional. Do you call that a beating? Sometimes, I suppose it was. But I got the belt all the time, yes, and the fact that I did was neither here nor there. It wasn't like I was the only one getting beaten in our neighborhood. Nobody was saying, "Poor John. He gets the belt." Every kid was getting the same shit.

Meanwhile, my relationship with my mother was always good. She was a very hard-working, long-suffering woman typical of that generation. She went to church every Sunday and worked at the bank part-time. She was charismatic, joyful, and social. Her bridge club met in our house every Wednesday afternoon. My mother was a good woman, and on reflection, I never really understood the love she clearly had for my father.

ME: What did you learn from having to preempt your father's moods?

John McAfee: By the time I was twelve, I could tell by the sound my father's shoes made when he walked across the hall what kind of mood he was in. Accordingly, I'd either be jovial with him, or I'd just pick up my books and go to my room. I instinctively knew which to do and when.

And my point is that, once you've learned how to read one person, you definitely notice how valuable that ability is as a tool in all human relationships. I was never the biggest, the strongest, or the fastest kid in my neighborhood. But I was the boss of every fucking neighborhood I ever lived in because I became adept at reading people and treating them accordingly.

The same applied to every company I've ever worked in. I have applied these abilities to understand what makes another person tick ever since childhood and have always treated people the same no matter what because of that. Even today, if a derelict dude comes up to me in the street, I'll give him money. But at the same time, I'll look into his eyes and have a conversation, assuming one is possible. It's all the same to me. I have never in my life judged anyone.

ME: Would you describe these years in Salem, Virginia, as happy?

John McAfee: We moved to Salem from Bristol, Tennessee, when I was six, and we stayed there until I was nineteen and left home to go to college in Roanoke. And I would say that, in spite of my father's moods, these were the happiest days of my life.

Our house was right beside the woods, and when we reached a certain level of maturity, we were given the freedom to cycle into the woods, build tree houses, and, at times, camp out there for an entire weekend at a time. Obviously, we'd have to check in at home every once in a while, or we voluntarily came back because we needed something trivial like more milk. But generally, I remember having this real sense of liberation in that house. If you summed the whole time up, it was idyllic.

ME: Did you do well in school?

John McAfee: I wouldn't say I was especially smart, but I did what the teachers told me to do. Basically, I obeyed, and, again, I learned this as a result of having to figure my own father out. When someone is older than you, outweighs you by a factor of ten, you do exactly what they tell you to do. Metaphorically, within that system, teachers represented the same thing. They could punish me, expel me, and call the police or whatever. I didn't want any of that, so I did exactly what I was told, but no more. I didn't study, never did homework. But when it came to the tests, I aced every single one of them.

ME: Were you made to go to church?

John McAfee: Oh, fuck yes—the Episcopal Church. I was a mini-Catholic. I sang in the choir; I was an altar boy too. I went to Sunday school. *The Book of Common Prayer* I could recite verbatim, and I don't know why because it's all utter nonsense.

Even at seven years old, I was questioning what God was, not because of religion per se, but because I was asking myself, "What the fuck is this thing—life—that I'm in?"

I mean, you appear on Earth at the age of zero, gain some semblance of consciousness at the age of two, and then there you are on a fucking scooter in your parent's yard at the age of seven thinking, *What the fuck am I even doing here?* At the time, I genuinely thought about these things with whatever capacity I had at the time. I've questioned everything about life ever since, including my own perceptions.

ME: Women—lots of them—have been a big part of your life. Do you remember when you were first alerted to the attractions of the opposite sex?

John McAfee: It's true. It would be impossible to tell my story without explaining the framework where women fit in. And I'm about to move outside to continue this talk because it's a conversation where the words I'm about to say should not be allowed to reverberate around inside a closed space. They need air.

I kissed my first woman when I was eight years old. The girl who sat beside me in class was the daughter of a dentist, and I remember that she had these blue jeans that, when she folded them up, you could see the Scottish plaid lining on the inside. I thought they were the cutest. I thought she was cuter.

One afternoon, I followed her home through the woods between school and where she lived. We all walked home; it was this tiny little town. I ran up to her, kissed her on the cheek, and then ran away. Good God, that was the most thrilling moment of my life up until that time—and perhaps even now. Even in my most drugged-out states in later life, I don't think I've ever recaptured the divinity of what I experienced that day.

ME: How did you feel in that precise moment?

John McAfee: You want to talk about a surge of emotion and love—this was it. There was absolutely no sexual attachment to this event, but I did feel desire of some kind. I received a momentary glimpse into an adult world that obviously I didn't understand. The thrill that I felt in that one-eighth of a second peck on the cheek was like a bolt of lightning that showed me what life might be like. At the moment my lips touched her skin, I thought, *OK, this is where I'm headed.*

ME: How did she respond?

JOHN MCAFEE: It's hard to say because I ran off so fast! Just grabbed a kiss and ran. But I don't think she reacted in any way negatively. Some would say that that was my first criminal act: molestation. You know that it would be called that today. And I'm willing to talk about it openly. If anyone has a problem with it, we are in serious trouble.

ME: What was your next experience with a woman?

JOHN MCAFEE: Well, as I grew older, I started becoming much more aware of sex and that our purpose on this planet is to propagate. Obviously, there was no internet back then, but we did have occasional access to a copy or two of my dad's *Playboy* magazines, which we all sat around and shared in our teenage years. That was our Pornhub.

Playboy magazine aside, there was nothing to do in that tiny town. There was a school, three restaurants, and an amusement park that was closed all winter. But there was a skating rink within walking distance of our houses, and I was one of the few in my peer group who got into skating at all. It was considered pretty dorky by my friends in those days. But the way I saw it, it wasn't them I was trying to fuck. No, I had noticed that, if you wanted to find girls, they were most likely at that goddamn skating rink. So I got pretty good, to the extent that I could skate backward, talking, etc., and could then fly by a girl, wink, or say something complimentary like, "My, I like how you've fixed your hair."

ME: And the sexual experience was at the skating rink?

JOHN MCAFEE: No, but it was this place that led me down the path of my actual sexual experience at the age of fifteen, with a twenty-one-year-old woman named Jill. She was extremely attractive, and I met her at the skating rink.

But the problem was that she was engaged to an older man. Regardless, the truth of the matter is that she got me involved in her life as opposed to me gatecrashing hers. At first, she got me involved in her church. It was the summer of 1960; all of us were off school. Meanwhile, her boyfriend had a regular job and was at work every day while she sat around at home all week with nothing to do.

It started with her taking me for drives in her car. And then those drives in the car turned into us parking the car somewhere and kissing. She and I just burned up the month of June. We were going out almost every day and doing this. It was such a great time.

ME: Did it go further?

John McAfee: It took me weeks to pluck up the courage to touch this woman at all. Also, because of her religious beliefs, she was still a virgin, albeit she was engaged to this guy and had been for months, possibly even years.

However, one night, a month or so after we started kissing, her fiancé had to go to Richmond for the weekend. So we went out to a drive-in movie in her car. Meanwhile, my mother was extremely concerned about all this—"What are you doing with this woman, going out at night?" She was very conservative in that sense. If she'd had her way, I'd still be a virgin today. However, that night in the car, we went all the way. I took her from behind in the back seat.

Back in those days, there was something called a party line, where maybe a hundred people in the neighborhood could share a phone line by jumping on and off. Obviously, there was no privacy. People used it to spy on what their neighbors were saying and doing.

Well, later that night, Jill called, and we talked, specifically about some of the acts we'd performed earlier that evening—"I loved it when you did me from behind," etc. The problem was the brother of a friend of mine heard all of this and immediately told Jill's fiancé.

ME: Was that the end of the affair?

John McAfee: At church the following Wednesday, it all came out. I was there, Jill was there with her fiancé, and my friend's brother was asked to lead the prayer that night. He stood up and said, "I need a private prayer with John." He also requested that Jill's fiancé be there too, and let's just say that he was one angry motherfucker at this point. But my friend's brother took control of the situation, simply because his younger brother, with whom I'd built tree houses while growing up, had said, "Don't let him kill my friend John." My friend's brother, who was a mean motherfucker himself, just said words to the effect of, "It ends tonight. And from now on, you need to be more careful." My first love affair was over, and that, at the time, was an absolute tragedy.

ME: Did this first experience with the opposite sex spur you on to discover more?

JOHN MCAFEE: It took me a month to summon up the courage to even go back to the skating rink. I never saw Jill there again, but another girl, Annie, an excellent skater herself, was second in line for my eyes. A couple of weeks later, she and I had sex, and that started a sequence of conquests—possibly fifteen or so—all in this little town.

By the next year, I'd lost count of how many women I'd slept with, but one of them of particular note was Sue. She was as cute as hell but also one of the freest women I'd ever met. She was way above me in terms of understanding herself. She was just such a wild bitch; we had wild sex exclusively in cars. And she also got me into stealing!

ME: Had you ever stolen before? Were you stealing for any particular reason?

JOHN MCAFEE: I hadn't, and it was just for the thrill of it all. She didn't need the items she stole or money; her parents were very well off. But her specialty was stealing small items like silver spoons from antique stores in neighboring towns, which tended to be looked after by one person who could easily be distracted. The act of stealing was just so exciting to me, even though we never did anything with the stuff we stole.

Later we got into stealing bicycles, which was a lot scarier and much more dangerous. Instead of stealing from antique stores from under the noses of eighty-year-old lady proprietors who looked at me as if I was their sweet grandson, now we were going to residences and stealing bikes from garages and off front porches—a whole different ball game that was.

Eventually, we literally had a basement full of fucking bicycles, to the point where Sue's dad kept saying, "Where are these coming from?" "Oh, John has a new bicycle repair business," she told him. Some we gave away; others we even took back—but not to the people we had stolen them from. Trying to take them back was every bit as much fun. We'd go into neighborhoods at two o'clock in the morning, look at a house and say, "It looks like kids live here," and then we'd just leave a bike on the porch and drive away. We could fit four bikes in the car at once.

ME: Did you ever get caught?

John McAfee: No, of course not. We were two smart kids, sixteen or seventeen years old. We were never going to get caught. We also started breaking into parked cars, which was obviously different in those days before central locking. By creeping around baseball stadium parking lots a hundred miles away, where nobody knew us or had ever seen us, and where we knew nobody would be watching, we had our way many times. You wouldn't believe what we collected: cameras, binoculars...cash. None of it was ever put to any use.

But again, it was the most fun I'd ever had, and furthermore, it made me realize that if you don't secure your shit in life, you do not deserve that shit. There is always going to be someone out there, like Sue and I were back then, who is ready to take it from you. That's what some young people do. They just want thrills. And believe me, there is no bigger thrill than risking your entire reputation by doing something that you know society is going to universally condemn.

Imagine how that old lady in the antique store, who once looked at you like her grandson, would look at you if she knew that you had her silver spoons in your pocket. That's a big fucking risk to take on every level, but, for me, it was a risk worth taking. It was physically arousing. While doing this, I'd inevitably get erections, and Sarah would often get wet, so we'd park the car somewhere, run into the woods, and fuck like wild bears.

ME: Was there a special one among these early girlfriends?

John McAfee: Without question, a girl called Alexa, who I also met at the Episcopal Church in Salem, although she actually came from nearby Roanoke. Meanwhile, my family could only be described as very sub-middle class in the sense that my parents, even when my dad was still around, never had much in the way of wealth. Right from the start, this was a problem with Alexa's parents. She personally didn't care, but her parents certainly didn't want her running around with someone as low class as they thought I was.

We started an affair that lasted for a number of years. It wasn't ever an exclusive arrangement—certainly not as far as I was concerned—but whenever she was home for vacations, we would get together. I would park my mother's car up the hill from her house around midnight and sneak through backyards and into Alexa's bedroom via her by then opened window, where we'd have endless, silent sex all night long.

ME: Was there something specific that attracted drew you to Alexa?

John McAfee: She was smart, and she was also a fucking rebel. Now, if you can find a rich girl who is also a rebel, you are onto something, my friend. This relationship continued into my first year in college, when she was attending school up in Washington, DC. Thereafter, she resurfaced many times over the years until as recently as thirty years ago. It was all so long ago. Fuck me, time flies so fast, Mark. How old are you, my friend?

ME: I'm almost fifty.

John McAfee: Ah, that age of transition of thought, where you go from looking forward to looking backward. When you get to my age, when you look forward, there isn't much there. But when you look back, there's a wealth of experience and information. That experience is important to reflect on for any person. Some people never do it; others do it constantly. The latter is the group of people I want to be with and talk to. Often, I can learn more by looking into someone's eyes than from anything that they say.

For a few minutes, we detoured in one of those wistful moments I enjoyed most with McAfee. It was during these periods of reflection where his eyes were at their kindest and simultaneously their saddest. McAfee, for all his bravado, definitely could be vulnerable.

I could sense that this was a man who had lived a fulfilling life but also one who had deep regrets and pain about aspects that he knew he could never hope to fix. I knew that the relationship he had with his father was a subject that he'd rarely talked about in interviews over the years. I wanted to tread carefully on it out of respect for his feelings. But at the same time, I knew that his father was one of the most significant people in his life, not because he showed love or was inspiring in any way, but because he informed almost all of McAfee's behaviors in later life.

ME: I know how sensitive this is, but how did your father's suicide affect you?

John McAfee: I was fifteen at the time, and I'm going to have to be really honest with you here. It felt pretty good.

Don't get me wrong, I cried. I wasn't the kind of kid who laughed at funerals. And at that time, I felt hurt because he was no longer in my life. But at the same time, there was this other part of me that was saying, "Dude, do you understand what this *means*?"

It was *freedom.* My dad represented the last thing that was ever going to control any part of my life. By that point, I had teachers wrapped around my finger and my mother the same. Dealing with my father had trained me well in terms of how to predict what people might want now, or in two minutes or in two hours. And now that he was gone, there was nobody left who was controlling me, and in the case of teachers, they didn't need to anyway as I was already obedient. It sounds strange probably, but I really saw my dad's death, as much as it was the end of his life, as the beginning of mine at the time.

ME: How do you feel about your father nowadays?

John McAfee: Well, I'll say this much: my father has been a looming presence in my entire life in a way that I didn't expect when I was fifteen. He's been with me every day since the day he died. Every situation of mistrust I find myself in, he is the sole negotiator of that mistrust. As much as I never truly felt his love, he has never gone away.

ME: What did this sense of liberty that you felt after your father died make you want to do with your life thereafter?

John McAfee: I wouldn't say that I had any clear aspirations in high school, but I definitely knew what I liked. The sciences interested me. Chemistry, biology, physics. Of the three, physics was my greatest love, and because of that affinity, I ended up going to nearby Roanoke College on a physics scholarship in September of 1963.

However, my issue was and has always been laziness. Laziness has killed every ambition I've ever had in my life. Even McAfee Associates years later, I never really wanted to do. It just kind of happened. But in my first semester at college, I found myself looking around and thinking, *Goddamn, there are a lot of classes.* Not only that, I discovered that in order to get a physics degree, I also had to take every fucking math class that I would have to take to get a math degree. I thought, *Fuck this. I'm just doing math.*

ME: Path of least resistance? I'm assuming you found math easy?

John McAfee: I have always approached everything in life from a mathematical perspective, including relationships. Everything to me is formulaic in some way, and even as a college student, I didn't have to work at any of it. It was all in my head.

So, there I was at college, with a curriculum that would get me a fucking degree and then a job, and to get all that, I didn't have to do a fucking ounce of work. In high school, if you didn't show up to class, you got suspended. But at college, nobody fucking cared. Every now and then, I would check in to make sure I wasn't completely self-deluded in what was happening, but in general, I sailed through. I never once showed up to class. I had fallen into the Garden of Eden.

My first semester in pure math, I got straight As, having done not a stroke of work. All I ever did was read the textbooks, which, incidentally, is something nobody else ever did. They showed up to class, hoping that the professor would somehow impart the knowledge to them either by force or osmosis. All they needed to do was read the fucking textbook. My view was always, "Why would I need that sonofabitch to teach me when all he's done is read this shit to be able to teach me? Fuck him—I'll read this myself!" Mostly it took me less than a day to read the entire book anyway. I could solve the math problems in a matter of minutes.

ME: I assumed you partied at college.

John McAfee: Hell yes. I drank like crazy. I had never really drunk in high school so you could say I was a late starter but a quick learner. I never did a lick of work, had my own apartment on campus, and I had a whole series of entrepreneurial jobs that I did to make a fortune on the side.

The best of them was a subscription sales job with a company called Ben Franklin Magazines. In these days, long before the internet, this company had created a moneymaking paradigm selling magazines in the mail. They made no money whatsoever from the magazine subscriptions themselves, but they did make money through advertising. And that advertising was based on the number of subscribers. If you had half a million readers, you were in fat city; the productions costs were next to nothing.

So Ben Franklin Magazines went to all the major titles, *Homes & Gardens, Men's Journal, Field & Stream,* etc., and said, "If we can get you real subscribers and prove that they have paid, will you give us the magazines for free?" They said something along the lines of, "Of course. But you can't do that shit!" Ben Franklin Magazines said, "Just watch us...."

ME: Where did you fit into all of this?

John McAfee: Well, this buddy of mine told me about this job going door-to-door selling these subscriptions, and he said, "Dude, you would be perfect for this."

I went to their offices in Roanoke, and when I walked in, there was basically this warehouse with hundreds of women on the phone. I got taken into the office and had the system explained, all of which began with these women on the phone. "Hello, Mrs. Jones? This is Katherine from Ben Franklin Magazines. Mrs. Jones, have you ever won anything before?" "Why no…." "Well, you might want to sit down because you have just won a five-year free subscription to any magazine of your choice. I know you are having a hard time believing this, so we are going to send our route manager out to you tomorrow to give you your guarantee."

I became one of two dozen of these route managers, and I came into the office whenever the fuck I wanted every day and said, "OK, what leads have you got?" Then I'd go out, college dude, charismatic smile, etc., knock on the door and say, "Mrs. Jones, John McAfee from Ben Franklin Magazines. I just want to say congratulations. And by the way, can I come in?"

ME: I'm guessing being a salesman came naturally to you?

John McAfee: Of course! I'd get invited in, offered tea or coffee, and then from there, I'd explain that, while the magazines were absolutely free, we asked that the customer only paid the mailing charges, which amounted to eighty-four cents per week.

"Now, Mrs. Jones, you don't want to have to write a check for eighty-four cents a week for five years, do you? That would be 250 checks. Wouldn't it be easier to just write a check for the full amount today?"

Meanwhile, while I'm saying this, I'm pulling out this great foldout display of all the magazines available, and she's saying, "Oh my, you have knitting magazines!" and I'm thinking, *Yeah? Who gives a shit?*

Well, maybe two out of ten people would write me a check there and then for the full amount. Others would choose the payment plan that allowed two payments, and the rest would pay one-fifth annually. I was guaranteed to get to keep that one-fifth check every time I went out.

ME: Did you ever run into any problems?

John McAfee: Occasionally, I'd get a husband who'd answer the door and say, "Why don't you get an honest goddamn job?" That would happen now and again. It was pointless showing up on the weekend to deal with some husband, the guy who was earning the money and knew the real value of it. No, I needed to speak to the wives, sitting at home bored out of their minds every day, wanting some free magazines. I just adapted and made sure I showed up on weekdays.

ME: How lucrative was this operation?

John McAfee: I probably closed six deals every time I went out. That amounted to around $300 a day. Meanwhile, I was a fucking college student whose apartment only cost sixty dollars a month! You can figure that out, my friend. I had more money than I knew what to do with, and before long, I went straight out and bought a brand new MGB sports car. I paid $3,000 in cash.

And that wasn't even the most lucrative job I had. At one point, I set myself up as an interior designer without actually knowing anything about design per se. Nevertheless, I had a good eye for how things could be. I read some books, figured it out, and because there were no other interior designers in Roanoke at the time, I landed enough jobs to make almost $30,000 in a year. And the work was good. I have always had a good design ethic.

ME: So you weren't exactly living the standard college student life?

John McAfee: You're not kidding. I had a sports car, was living not in a fucking frat house but in my own pad, and was getting more pussy than God. I was totally free from all the normal nonsense of college—all that dorm room shit and stupid regulations about when I could come and go.

And because I never went to class, I basically had free time twenty-four hours of the day until exam time or term paper time came. I could do what I wanted whenever I wanted, and that became the theme for my entire life. From the age of seventeen, all I have ever wanted is to just be me. I didn't want fucking rules because they told me to be something other than me. At some point they tried to induct me into some kind of rules-based stupid fraternity, but I just walked away from that shit. The rules for being me were rules only I could make.

ME: Did you apply this mode of thinking to every aspect of your life thereafter?

John McAfee: I challenge you to find a single thing I have ever done that does not adhere to that principle.

ME: You mentioned you still saw Alexa while you were at college?

John McAfee: I did, but while I was at poor man's school, she was at one of the better schools, just outside Washington, DC. So, every Friday, I used to drive up there in my MGB, and she'd sneak out of school to spend the entire weekend with me. We'd check into a motel somewhere and just go and party in Georgetown. Sometimes we didn't sleep for forty-eight hours. It was heavenly, but this part of the story is sad for me to relate even today.

Her parents hired private detectives, and they found out that she and I had been seeing each other. They then forced her to tell me that it was over, and she did so one Sunday as we were driving back from Washington. I was heartbroken. I had to have my head out the car window while we were driving because I just couldn't breathe because of the overall sense of sadness.

I was despondent for weeks. I tried to call, but all the numbers had been changed. I couldn't have exactly shown up at her house either. Her father was a powerful man and might well have had me whacked. It would be years until we were in contact again, but by the time we did, the mad attraction that we shared as teenagers was no longer there.

THREE

DARK SIDE OF THE MOON

The following week, I started feeling an increasing sense of warmth from Mr. McAfee. As much as we'd talked about him, and as much as he'd clearly relished the process of getting some early childhood memories off his chest, I always felt that it was a one-way process. One-way, when you're trying to write a book about someone else's life is usually how it has to be. There is, of course, little time for anything else, as much as a bit of mutual understanding certainly helps the collaborative process.

However, if there was one thing I'd learned about McAfee in the few weeks that we'd been talking, it was that, as much as he had lived his life his own way, often to his detriment, other people were as much a part of the story as he was. He needed wives, many of them, and twice as many girlfriends and mistresses. He had friends, at various levels. But more than either of those, he appeared to have a curiosity about and, ultimately, an affinity with total strangers he encountered, of which I was one.

"Tell me, how well do you play the guitar, my friend?" he asked at the beginning of one of our calls, when he caught sight of a guitar in the background in my office.

"Not well," I said, "I've tried at various times in my life to improve but have rarely had the time."

"What do you think of musicians like Peter Frampton and Eric Clapton?" he asked.

"I like them. I'm a big fan of '70s music generally," I said.

"I think Peter Frampton's 'Do You Feel Like We Do' is the pinnacle of guitar mastery from that age," McAfee told me. "I have never heard anything quite like it."

"I wouldn't disagree with that," I replied, wondering where the conversation was going.

"It is still as fresh as it ever was, and in fact, I'm going to use it as background music for the first video for my 2020 presidential election campaign," he explained.

So that's where this was going, I thought to myself.

"I'm having these people put together a video that'll be a compilation of every aspect of me: playing the piano, on the stage at the Libertarian National Convention, drunk, on a jet-ski, carrying a bunch of weapons, smoking dope; I want this clip to be the complete package of me," he explained.

"Sure, what's the point of it all?" I asked.

"Well, obviously, I'm not running for president. Everybody knows that. But I do want the national stage. But, if I was running for president, I'd want them to know the bad as well as the good about me."

I think what McAfee was trying to tell me was, on one hand, that he had many qualities that he saw as being worthy of illustrating: kind, funny, a great business manager, an engaging public speaker, and so on. He was indeed all of these things. But on the other, he was telling me that he also knew what his own weaknesses were: a hard partier, lazy, an accomplished liar, a serial womanizer, and all the rest.

What this revealing conversation made me think was that, while McAfee was undoubtedly an accomplished liar when required, or at the very least a habitual distorter of the truth, there was also a big part of him that, at the age of seventy-four, badly needed the truth out there about his life.

While a twelve-minute campaign video for a mythical presidential run was one way of doing it, it also suggested to me that he saw our conversations, and the book that would result from them, as his one last chance at the truth, or at least as much of the truth as he was willing to part with. Having bailed on several other attempts to write about his life, why would he be bothering with our talks if he didn't really want people to know about him and understand what made him tick?

"So on that basis, if you're willing to show all sides of you in a campaign video, does the same apply to our conversations?" I asked him.

"Of course. Unless there are immediate and terrible repercussions associated with anything I tell you, what you will get is total honesty. The only situation in which I'll have to be economical is if something I say could materially harm someone else. I don't want to do that. Anything else...I don't care."

"How do I know that you're telling me the truth?" I asked.

"I'm seventy-four years old, my friend. At this point in life, I have no possible reason to do anything else," he replied.

With that, we proceeded.

ME: I assume you graduated from Roanoke College on time?

John McAfee: Yes, I graduated in 1967 and soon took up a funded graduation assistantship program place at North East Louisiana State University in the fall of 1968. Here I would be teaching math classes to undergraduates while simultaneously studying for my own master's degree in mathematics.

ME: Did teaching come naturally to you?

John McAfee: It's hard to say. Shortly after I arrived in Monroe, Louisiana, I met one of my students, Lindsay, who sat in the front row of my class. She was this beautiful young blond girl with nice legs. It didn't take long—like, fifteen minutes after the first class—for her to join me in bed. Before I could even finish my first quarter, I was thrown out of my assistantship for sleeping with one of my students.

Remember, this was the South in 1968, an era of repressed sexuality and extreme morality. Teachers did not just casually sleep with their students and get away with it. I lost my assistantship, and with no willingness to pay my own way through an expensive college, I went back to Virginia, whereupon I enrolled at Virginia Polytechnic Institute in Blacksburg for the next quarter, which was fifty miles from where I had been living in Roanoke.

ME: What happened to Lindsay?

John McAfee: After less than a month, Lindsay came to Virginia to live with me. And from here, my life started getting very complex.

I had only attended class at Blacksburg for one quarter before I got a job with General Electric in Roanoke as a programmer trainee. I took the job just for a summer, and I'm eternally grateful that I did. This was to be my first-ever exposure to computers.

ME: What did the computers look like in 1969?

John McAfee: Number one, they were huge. They'd fill an entire room. By today's standards, they had zero power. However, even in 1969, they had immense power in comparison to the human brain in terms of their power to process information.

Very quickly, I learned some very low-level but extremely important concepts about how hardware interfaced with software because I was working on something called process automation. Process automation was pretty much all that General Electric did at that time, and it was specifically designed for factories, canning companies, steel mills, and so on. And so, I was tasked to create the system that automated Australia Iron & Steel's rolling mill in Port Kembla, New South Wales. Unfortunately, I did not get to finish that job because the end of the summer came, and I started looking at my life and what I wanted to do with it.

ME: What conclusions did you reach?

John McAfee: One thing I was certain about was that I didn't want to go back to school. What I had learned in three months at General Electric was so much more valuable than the entirety of my college education up to that point. Computer programming is just math. Computers at that time were mathematics in a world where only two numbers, zero and one, mattered. Now, it really didn't matter what the numbers were. It was all still mathematics. Ten, twenty, or sixteen—like hexadecimal, one of the computer concepts—it wasn't important. To me, it was just a piece of cake, and the difference was because it was a job, I actually had to be there and apply myself every day.

I learned more in those three months than I ever did at any other time in my life. And I didn't just do eight hours a day. No. I went home at night and started playing with the computer instructions, finding out how everything worked. I was fascinated. I was drawn in by an absolutely random summer job. It was the fulcrum point of my life.

ME: Did you ever go back to Blacksburg?

John McAfee: At the time when I was meant to go back, I sat down and said to myself, *Wait a minute. I have achieved more in computer science in a little town in Virginia than I ever could have elsewhere.*

This was all true. However, as much as I'd mastered some of the principles of process automation, I also knew that process automation itself was only a tiny corner of computer science, even as it existed at that time. I yearned for more, so what I did was think of the company I most wanted to work for in the whole world. And the first name that sprang to mind was NASA, the National Aeronautics and Space Administration. I was a science nut with a taste for fantasy. What other company was going to fit the bill?

ME: True, but this sounds like an ambitious idea for a guy with just three months' experience at General Electric.

John McAfee: It was, and I didn't just want to work at NASA; I wanted to work at the Institute for Space Studies, which was located on the campus of Columbia University in Manhattan, New York City.

So, I dummied up a resume that gave me three years more experience than I actually had, sent it in, and, lo and behold, I scored an interview. I had lied, true, but I also banked on them not checking my references, just for the purposes of an initial interview. I thought, *Why would they fucking bother*? It was a risk worth taking. I just wanted to get myself in the fucking door so that I could sit down in front of the person who was going to say yes or no. If I could get that far, I knew I had the ability, and the charisma, to get that job. And that's exactly what happened.

ME: How, exactly, did you wing an interview at NASA?

JOHN MCAFEE: I was asked some serious shit in that interview, but thank God, it was all stuff that I could answer coherently at the time. Not only could I answer these questions, but I found a way to add to these solutions by offering further ideas and suggestions. They must have been sitting there thinking, *Hell, we had never even thought of that.*

ME: Did they ever check your references?

JOHN MCAFEE: Either they didn't check them as I hoped they wouldn't. Or they did check them, and it didn't fucking matter that they were bogus because I so blew away the interviewer that they couldn't *not* give me that job.

Anyhow, within days, I was packing up my shit and moving to New York City, while the girl, Lindsay, reluctant to make the big change in lifestyle, went back to Louisiana.

I found myself an apartment, started the job, and for one solid year and a half, I was in heaven. I was working with not only the top minds in New York or even America, but also the top minds in the fucking world were right there with me—the people who were planning the mission to the moon, missions to Mars, and planning our entire satellite program. All of the most senior architects were right there, and I felt like I was in fat city because I was part of it.

ME: Having got the job by lying, how did you manage to keep winging it?

John McAfee: Yes, I had the capability, and I'd proved that during the interview and kept proving myself thereafter. My first job within the program was related to the Tiros 1 weather satellite, which had been up in space since its launch in April 1960. Ever since then, for almost ten years, it had been sending back data nonstop, twenty-four hours of every day. But we did not have the technology to process any of this data properly.

And then the IBM 360 came out, the first general-purpose, large-scale computer. It had about the power that the average smartphone has today, but instead of being six inches long, it covered almost an entire floor of a massive building. That was my tool. Then they gave me all the data from Tiros 1 and said, "Is there anything that can be done here? We haven't figured out how to process all of this yet."

ME: So what did you do to solve their problem?

John McAfee: Well, the first thing I thought was, *What am I fucking going to do with this?* Half of this data was coming back in pre-digital—analog—form. There were *years* of this stuff. The task seemed overwhelming. But the first thing I actually did was spend a week taking drugs and walking the streets of New York City, day and night.

ME: Why drugs, and why then?

John McAfee: This was 1969, arguably the most symbolic year of all for drug experimentation. I was in New York when Woodstock was happening. Everybody was talking about it; everybody was curious about drugs. I'd already done a bunch of drugs before 1969. I'd already tried LSD and all manner of other psychedelics. For me, drugs, no matter what they were, put me in a different state of perspective. I'm not saying it was always the proper state or even a real state, but, equally, sometimes it was. So I spent that week just sleeping little, cogitating, drawing schematics, writing notes, and then, finally, "Ha! It's a piece of cake!" I had the solution.

I then went back to my office, wrote a program, presented it, and that program is still cranking away at the Tiros 1 weather satellite today as we speak. My Tiros 1 work got me the accolades to write my own ticket to any programming job I ever wanted. And, in the short term, it proved to my bosses at NASA that I was legitimate, which meant I could keep the job as long as I wanted it. Unfortunately, it turned out only to be for a year and a half.

ME: Why? What happened?

John McAfee: Well, Lindsay, the girl who had left, had come to New York a few times to see me and had gotten pregnant. Allegedly, it was my kid, she said. And at that time, because we didn't have synthetic paternity testing, a man just had to take the woman's word for it. Regardless, whether the child was mine or not was immaterial. I stepped up, left New York, where I'd made a lot of money, and moved to Tennessee to marry Lindsay, have a family, and, in theory, to start a completely new life.

ME: Was there a particular reason you chose Tennessee?

John McAfee: Bear in mind, at this point, I was walking around with a serious NASA resume. Programmers, in 1970, were absolute the gods of money. We were some of the highest-paid people in the professional world, assuming that you consider programming to be a professional occupation. We could ask anything of anybody at that time. I could have got any job I wanted.

Univac, a company that hasn't existed since the late 1980s, was the second-largest computer company in America at that time. And their engineering and development plant was in Bristol, Tennessee, which also happened to be where my mother lived at the time. Bristol is a strange concept. Half of it is in Tennessee; the other half is in Virginia. One city, two states.

Anyway, there I was in Bristol, Tennessee, married with a young baby daughter, and I started working at Univac. Like I had at NASA, I did a great job, and it was there that I finally learned how to write operating systems for computers, the fundamental underlying "brain" on top of which all applications, etc., ran. Back in those days, this was laborious, complicated work. Even to get something to print, a whole program had to be written just to be able to interface with a printer at all. Those programs then became part of the operating system.

ME: So are we talking about the era of the C prompt here?

John McAfee: (laughter). The C prompt didn't appear until we had actual computer screens, where we could actually see something on there using a keyboard. It would be another twenty-five years until that shit hit the world, and it only existed in its capacity as an icon for Microsoft's DOS operating system anyway.

I was working on front panels on these machines in 1970. I literally threw switches on and off. It was primitive work. Then a little later, we got punch cards, and boy did that feel like a miracle. Instead of writing a program out in machine code and then going to the front panel to set the switches according to these instructions, punch cards allowed you to write these instructions out—and these weren't instructions like "print"; these were "if A +B," etc.—and then you could just feed those cards into the computer, and the instructions could be set from the cards. This was one of the biggest advancements in computer programmer interfaces.

ME: Were you happy in this new family setup?

John McAfee: Wait a minute. You're getting a little deeper than I thought you were going to get today.

ME: It's not especially deep. It was a straightforward question. Do you not want to talk about it?

John McAfee: OK, well, like all people, the answer was yes and no. Of course, no matter where we are, we make our own happiness. I've been in jails and prisons, and I've seen people in there make their own happiness. So a better question might have been, "Would I have changed my situation had I had the courage?"

ME: That's fine. Why not answer that question instead?

John McAfee: Yes, I would have changed it, absolutely. For a while, everything was fine. And then, things weren't fine, simply because Tennessee was not Manhattan. The culture I'd acclimated myself to for that year and a half was the total opposite of Tennessee, the nature of which was reserved with a very fundamental Christian set of moralities.

The truth of the matter was that I was just not cut out to be tied down into a marriage where I was expected to conform to a set of norms that denied the better part of me, especially not in rural Tennessee as it was then. However, at the time, I accepted it, like we all accept what we think is the inevitable.

But these things are never really inevitable. As human beings, we are masters of our own ship. And that, my friend, is the only thing we are masters of. That was especially true of me. And any time I tried to be the master of anyone other than me, I only got fucked over royally. Interfering in other people's lives for my own benefit was something I never felt I had the right to do.

ME: Did you feel that this seemingly happy family life was temporary?

John McAfee: Well, I had a wife, my daughter, and a good job. On that level, things were fine. But as I mentioned earlier, the environment that I was in in Tennessee never really fit with the values that I had in 1971. And then, as if to confirm that, I got arrested for dealing drugs. It was a huge deal in the local newspapers, and given that this was Tennessee, my bosses at Univac took a very moralistic view of everything and fired me on the spot. This judgmental view came all the way down from the top, I was told.

Suddenly, I was jobless and facing the possibility of years in prison. So I contacted my attorney uncle, Carl McAfee, to represent me at trial, and somehow, thanks to him, the felony charges were dropped. Nevertheless, I was left with a misdemeanor for possession and still had to leave town in early 1972, pretty much with my tail between my legs.

ME: Why did you deal drugs at all when you had a well-paying job?

John McAfee: Habit? I don't fucking know. It was just fun for me, even to meet interesting people. Working at a place like Univac, I was working with folks who in no way had anything in common with me other than the work. So I dealt drugs to keep in touch with the underbelly of society, which is more than often the source of revolution, new ideas in politics, and everything else. I've always kept in touch with these folks.

ME: So you left town with your wife and daughter? What was the plan thereafter?

John McAfee: At this point, I definitely took my responsibilities seriously. We traveled to St. Louis, Missouri, where I took a job as programming manager for the Missouri Pacific Railroad, which was at that time automating all their rail car movements.

This was one of the biggest challenges in all of the industry. Even in 1972, they probably had ten thousand cars, all of them moving in different directions on different trains. My job was to automate all this so that the computer could work out the best and most economically efficient routes. As opposed to my work with Australia Iron & Steel, where we were automating the machinery based on feedback we were getting from the steel rollers, at Missouri Pacific Railroad, we were automating the *people* controlling the cars.

ME: Did you continue dealing drugs in St. Louis?

JOHN MCAFEE: I wasn't dealing so much, but I was certainly heavily into taking drugs at that time. I'd been taking all kinds of different shit and wasn't really feeling anything, so one night, in the apartment we were renting, I took an overdose of something my friends claimed was DMT, which was meant to be like a powerful, naturally occurring equivalent to LSD. All I really remember was that it was an orange color. It wasn't just a mild overdose either; this was massive.

The long and short of it was that I basically lost contact with all reality for three months. I lost my job, which was highly embarrassing. I lasted a few days, but it must have been apparent to everyone that I no longer knew what the function of my job was. The program might as well have been spitting out rail car routes to Mars.

Then, after about a week, when I walked in one morning, everybody was just staring at me. I don't know why. I don't think I was naked, but at that point, I could easily have been. But I must have looked crazy. A friend of mine who also worked at the company and had supplied me drugs at various times in the past was sent into my office to deal with me.

This dude talked to me for a while, established that he didn't need to call the police or to hospitalize me, and then calmly walked me to the door while everyone just stared. I got in my car, drove away, and that was the last I ever saw of the Pacific Railroad job. They had no choice but to fire me.

ME: Do you remember what it felt like when you took this drug?

JOHN MCAFEE: I was sitting around this table with these friends in the apartment. We all took a little; I assume everyone else was tripping. But initially, I didn't feel anything. Then I snorted a bit more, and then a bit more for good measure. I just kept doubling my dose until I felt something, because that's how I approach things. When the drug came on for real, the table started spinning in a DNA type of spiral going upwards. Then, we all climbed on top of this table, whereupon it shot up through the roof and into the stratosphere. We were all desperately just clinging onto this table. These were my perceptions of reality, and it got stranger from there. Honestly, it was three months until I could recognize a semblance of normality. Even today, I still struggle with it at times.

ME: What were you actually doing during these lost three months?

John McAfee: Eventually, unable to deal with me, Lindsay took our daughter and drove back to Virginia to stay with my mother. Meanwhile, I stuck out the aftermath of this trip alone in the apartment. I got crazy. And I mean scary crazy. That's how bad it was. People were calling and stopping by. Apparently, I hadn't shaved or showered for days or weeks.

Eventually, getting desperate, I called that old flame Alexa. I'd been calling her all the time, and eventually, she just said, "Don't worry, I'll come to St. Louis. You need help."

So, she came to St. Louis, and yes, I was married with a daughter, and yes, I was now cheating on my wife with an ex-girlfriend. However, one night, she and I were sitting on the sofa listening to Pink Floyd's *Dark Side of the Moon*, which is still one of my favorite albums today. It's hard to explain this, but as I was sitting there, I felt like I went through an entire lifetime before being shocked back to the sofa again. Then I went through another lifetime, and then I'd be shocked back to the sofa again.

At one point, I left Alexa and went out to downtown St. Louis. I have no idea why. I felt that everybody was after me or something bad was happening. Meanwhile, I was scurrying around, paranoid, hiding behind trash cans in back alleys. If anyone came anywhere near me, I'd dig deeper in.

Then, suddenly, from this position behind a dumpster, I had this feeling that I had to find a certain person, I don't know who. But I got it into my head that they might be in this bar around the corner. So I very slowly peered in the window of this bar and then backed up a little. And then I edged closer again. Pretty soon, people started looking at me, and when I finally summoned the courage to walk in the door, two people stood up!

I thought, *Fuck me. I'm in a dangerous situation here,* and instinctively picked up the phone book that was sitting beside the payphone at the door and started leafing through it. Lo and behold, it was no longer in alphabetical order. That's how fucked up I was. As I read these names, with G somehow before C, etc., I thought, *I have made a serious mistake. I have walked into a place of great evil.* I have no recollection of getting home that night.

That was just one episode. I lived multiple lifetimes, and I had flashbacks for years afterward, the most recent of which was in a bank in Woodland Park, Colorado, in 2004.

ME: What happened on that occasion?

John McAfee: I was standing in line, playing around with one of the little calculators. All of a sudden, I thought the digits on the calculator screen were showing my Social Security number, and in that moment, it felt like someone had tapped me on the shoulder, and I was right back in St. Louis, Missouri, on the sofa. I grabbed the podium and started screaming, "No! No!" all wild-eyed like an absolute madman.

The manager came out and ushered me into an office to calm down. Thank God I had millions of dollars at that time, or else I'd have probably been put in some kind of asylum. Anyway, gradually, I got a grip and realized that nothing bad was actually happening to me, by which time the busy bank had completely emptied, and I was then led back to the window to finish my business. That was the last time I flashed back in a major way.

ME: Knowing what you know about drugs, did this trip alter the wiring in your brain?

John McAfee: If it didn't, I don't know what the fuck was happening during those three months. The pivotal experience of all of this time was that I went through the most hellish periods of introspection. The drugs force you to do that shit. You are made to look at the raw, gory facts of you, and I don't mean the superficial shit you show to the world, where people might have looked at me and thought: *He's a nice guy, has a decent job, loves his family, has a kid….*

No—none of that shit was on the table. I had to look at the *real* me: the resentments, the flaws, the insecurities, the secret desires, and the twisted wishes that I'd never acknowledged. I had to live with all this for three fucking months.

ME: I've never taken drugs, so would you say psychedelics are synonymous with paranoia?

John McAfee: Not as a rule—no. It's usually stimulants: methamphetamines and, to a lesser extent, cocaine that will bring on paranoia. If you use crystal meth, for example, as I have done in recent years, you will develop severe paranoia within three or four months. Some people can deal with that; others can't. With psychedelics, massive overdoses and bad trips happen. I've gone through as many hellishly introspective trips as I have blissfully happy ones over the years.

ME: Would someone like me enjoy an LSD trip?

John McAfee: Well, it is a potluck what kind of trip you might have, which is why I don't recommend that anyone take drugs, even though I have at various times. And if you are insistent on experimenting with psychedelics, don't do it alone, and never do it with a stranger. Do it with somebody you know who has taken fifteen pounds of them and knows all of the potential outcomes. You need someone with you who knows the ropes a little and can recognize that when you're saying that you feel that you can fly and are standing on the edge of a roof about to try, they can say, "No, sir, you don't want to do that. Step down."

ME: Anyway, back to St. Louis. What happened after these lost three months?

John McAfee: Do I really want to tell you this? Well, OK, as long as you are giving me the right to review this at a later date.

ME: Sure. We'll decide whether it serves the story or not. But you make the ultimate call. It's your life.

John McAfee: At this point, I'd pretty much stopped taking my mother's calls because she didn't seem to be helping any. She'd been in almost constant contact, wondering what the fuck was going on with me. Then one day, I picked up, and she was pleading for me to come home. She made all kinds of assurances, promised that nobody was going to be judged, etc. So I agreed to go back.

However, bear in mind, I was still crazy. I was not in touch with reality whatsoever and, in fact, still doubted my own reality. I'd been so introspective for so long that I'd gone beyond myself and into the universe. I reached a point where I was crying because God, if there was a God, was alone.

I got in the car and started driving to Virginia, and I was so deranged that, when someone on the radio said, "Drink Coca-Cola," I immediately had to pull off the freeway and search for a place to buy a Coke. These weren't suggestions; these were commands. I genuinely believed that God was now talking to me through the car radio. That's how far off the map I was.

Along the way, I picked up two hitchhikers. I have no idea what I said or did, but within two or three minutes, they were fucking begging me to stop the car and let them out. I was on a fucking freeway at the time. There was nowhere to stop. "Please. Stop the car. Now." I hadn't threatened them; I didn't have a gun. I had nothing. But I clearly wasn't acting normally. But when I arrived in Bristol, I knew exactly what I was going to do.

ME: Which was?

John McAfee: I was going to kill my mother, my wife, and my baby daughter because God had told me to. It's important that you don't judge me here, my friend. In my mind, this was the only thing I could do.

ME: Are you serious? You were actually going to kill them?

John McAfee: At the time, that's what I felt compelled to do, yes. So I pulled into the driveway at my mother's house, on a nice quiet street in a nice rolling hills suburb of Bristol, Virginia, where there were lots of trees, grass, and flowers. I opened the door of the car, a white Chevrolet station wagon by the way, and as I got out, a man came walking across the yard straight toward me.

"Sir, do you believe that you have to be reborn into the kingdom of heaven?" he asked.

"Fuck, yes!" I said.

This was the first fucking person in three months that I actually felt like I could talk to. We went up on the porch and sat on the porch swing and talked.

Meanwhile, thank God my wife and mother had the common sense to leave it be and let me talk to this man. We swung for two hours while they looked out of the window at us from time to time, and for those two hours, he imparted the whole impact of the Holy Bible. In my perception at that time, and it wasn't a specifically Christian perception, everything he was saying made total sense.

ME: Why did this man's presence have so much impact at that time?

John McAfee: I don't know. I guess those two hours were all I needed. When he left, I didn't want his pamphlet, and I had no desire to either go to church or to go out on the street begging people to accept Christ into their lives. None of that shit appealed. All it did was get me to a place where I said to myself, *Was I really so crazy that I thought about killing my mother, my wife, and my daughter?* So I came into the house in peace. Confused as fuck? Yes. But I was at peace because I had connected with one other fucking human being who understood.

ME: Did you stay in Bristol?

John McAfee: I did for a while because being with my mother also gave me peace. My wife? Not so much. With hindsight, I think she was fucking with me. She'd say things like, "I just bought this beautiful picture of an owl today. Is it OK if I put it in our bedroom?" Well, what I saw was a picture not of an owl but of a fucking elephant. Many years later, I went back to check, and it was, indeed, an elephant. I don't know what her motives were, but that picture has always been an elephant.

ME: Did reality return gradually?

John McAfee: It certainly did not return overnight, my friend. In some senses, it is still returning to me even now, forty years later. However, I was in Bristol for a month or so until I reached a point where I felt I was able to put enough of the pieces of a new reality together to function somewhat. However, to continue to reassemble a new existence, I knew I had to be working.

I got a job working for Xerox in Rochester, New York. At that time, Xerox had been putting out computer systems, and it hadn't been going very well. So they hired me to develop the operating system for a new Xerox computer. I went to Rochester with my wife and daughter, was there for God knows how long, and it was during this time that I started gaining a degree of worldwide notoriety, not in the mainstream press, but in the upper echelons of the high-tech world.

ME: Was your marriage stable at this point?

John McAfee: Not especially, and that wasn't helped by the fact that Xerox wanted to send me to London to a branch where they were developing the hardware so that we could test the hardware and the software in the same place.

Initially, I had pushed back on the whole idea because my wife refused to go to London. I actually turned the job down to start with. "OK, how about we fly you back first-class every weekend so that you can spend them with your family?" "Fuck yes. I can do that," I told them. And for the next six months, I spent weekdays in London and weekends in Rochester.

And then my marriage fell apart, as marriages do. There were a variety of reasons, none of them significant. However, my wife took my daughter and moved back to Louisiana, while I quit Xerox and moved to California.

ME: Why California?

John McAfee: I wanted to live in LA. It was that simple. Everyone should live in LA at some point in his or her life if at all possible. So I got a job, and this is crazy, with The Great American Insurance Company, in an office where they were doing all their processing for their insurance policies.

In all honesty, I didn't particularly give a shit what the job was; I just wanted to go to LA, and they were willing to pay me a fortune and offer me an immediate start.

So now I was by myself. Well…not quite.

While I was living in London, I'd cultivated a love affair with a South African woman who worked in the South African embassy in Trafalgar Square. It wasn't long before she came to live with me in LA. Things were heavenly. That is, until the company decided to close the office and move the whole operation to their head office, which was located in Cincinnati, Ohio.

ME: Did you want to leave LA having just got there?

John McAfee: Hell no. However, I had not finished the job with the system they hired me to create, so as much as I didn't want to move to Cincinnati, I wanted to finish the job I'd started much more. I went to Cincinnati, rented a two-level, three-bedroom house in a nice suburb. It was a nice house; I was earning a fortune. Meanwhile, the lady from South Africa returned to South Africa. I then bought a motorcycle and started living the life of a free single man in his thirties.

ME: Until?

John McAfee: There is always that "until" moment, isn't there? Well, I was traveling on a bus one day, and I met this girl—Olivia, her name was. What I remember most about this meeting was that, while I was sitting behind her, I was just fascinated with her hair. It was like a lion's mane, and the whole energy that she emitted was like fire. She was three inches taller than me.

Obviously, we got together, and a couple of months later, we both decided, "Fuck the corporate world. This makes no sense." I had plenty of money, and we bought a van—a 1969 converted Chevrolet hippy van—with a bed, windows, and everything fixed up for living and traveling. We decided to go back to California. On the way, we really enjoyed this van life. We were smoking weed, taking other drugs, and then somehow, we ended up taking some major detours. And the next thing I knew, we were in fucking Mexico. At that point, I remember saying to Olivia, "You know, there's actually no hurry to get back to California…."

FOUR

DARWIN

In the days between the conversation about the events that occurred in St. Louis and, later, Bristol, Tennessee, I seem to recall that McAfee and I had some back and forth about whether it should be included in the book. His view was that it might reflect badly on him, a surprising viewpoint for someone so seemingly unconcerned about other people's opinions of him. Again, I wondered whether this feeling was because he knew that these conversations we were having, unlike others he'd had at various times, really were going to be published.

My humble view was that it would have reflected much worse on him had he actually killed his mother, daughter, and wife. Personally, I thought that the MDA overdose story was important, not just because it was gripping and unfathomable, but more because I hoped that it might serve as an illustrative baseline below which he'd never sink thereafter given that he would later quit taking drugs and alcohol for many years.

In the end, we agreed that the passage would remain. He didn't kill anyone. While an intention had been there, it came from a place of great confusion where he was completely detached from reality. In isolation, the story sounds horrendous. In context, we both felt that it made total sense. Obviously, it stayed in.

JOHN MCAFEE: A year later, we emerged, having been in jail twice and having had experiences beyond description, and me having read the entirety of Charles Darwin's *On the Origin of Species.*

ME: I'll come back to Darwin. Why were you in jail twice?

JOHN MCAFEE: We got to Mazatlán, this beautiful city by the beach that was popular with British and American tourists. It was a reasonably moneyed place, and the locals knew this, so they'd come around with these cases of beautiful jewelry, which you could buy affordably. A nice silver ring with a stone would only cost about twenty bucks, for example.

I found out where these stones came from—a place called Magdalena—and so we drove there, which took a couple of days, and after having made some contacts, we then went to Taxco, another thousand miles further south. This was the silk capital of Mexico, where all this jewelry was made. I bought rings, beautiful stones: fire agates, opals, aquamarines, etc., and then came up with the designs to give to the people in Taxco to make. Then I took the finished designs back to Mazatlán to sell to the stupid tourists at much higher prices than the locals were selling them.

ME: Was it a lucrative endeavor?

JOHN MCAFEE: Yeah, it went along pretty good for a while. I was also selling drugs here and there. Then we went to Puerto Vallarta, where the really rich people were.

On the first night we were there, we met an American couple who inevitably asked what I was doing in Mexico. I told them I was making bespoke jewelry, and then from there, I went into this whole spiel about why mine were the best quality, etc. "The ones you'll see the locals selling are tourist-level stones. Believe me, sir, these are gem-quality stones," I told them, and then went to get my jewelry case. I returned, opened the case, and was showing this guy my jewelry. I was about to make a $2,000 sale when two local policemen showed up. "Señor, we need you to come with us." We packed up the case, whereupon Olivia and I were arrested for selling jewelry without a license.

ME: Did you not know you needed a license?

John McAfee: Well, it might not sound like a big deal. But keep in mind that this was a tourist area where even the Mexican locals had to have permits. And to get one in the first place, they probably had to know somebody like the fucking mayor. And there I was, a goddamn gringo, selling shit to tourists. That was not going to be tolerated.

ME: How long were you in jail?

John McAfee: Let me first say that Mexican jails are great social meeting places. If you want a nice social club, check into a Mexican jail. You can get there easily too. Just pick a bar fight or whatever, and you'll end up in one soon enough. However, unless you're in Mexico City, the cells in Mexican jails are right next to the sergeant's desk. It's just tiny little halls with fourteen people in one goddamn cell.

As it turned out, we were probably only in there for half a day on this occasion. But while we were, I met this nice kid who spoke good English, and I was explaining to him what had happened and that the police, thinking we'd stolen this jewelry, wanted to see receipts, which of course we didn't fucking have. So this kid started talking to the sergeant, telling him that we'd just made a stupid mistake, didn't know any better, and that we hadn't stolen anything.

Eventually, they said they'd let us out, but on the condition that they kept the jewelry. "You're not keeping the gems," I said. There was this ten-minute standoff where I basically said, "Put me back in jail then. We'll let a judge decide who owns these fucking stones." In the end, they let us keep the gems on the condition that I never came back to Puerto Vallarta, which I never did.

ME: What happened the second time?

John McAfee: I had this motorcycle, which I attached to the back of the van on a rack. Whenever we arrived in a new place, I'd take the bike off and drive around the city. It was fun. Then the fucking rack broke in Mazatlán. Meanwhile, there was this American guy in one of the campgrounds we were staying at one night. He was kind of hard up and was living in a tent.

Bear in mind that I was a changed man at this point. Money and material things were of no consequence to me. So I gave him this motorcycle. Just gave it to him, a $2,000 motorcycle—it was a pretty hot bike, let me tell you. And then we just left thinking nothing more of it.

We continued driving around Mexico, and then at one point, we decided to leave Mexico and go into Belize. We would probably have left the country earlier, but Mexico is a big country, and we just hadn't stumbled upon a border previously. When we reached the border at Chetumal, they looked at our papers and said, "Sir, you have a van and a motorcycle listed on your papers. Where's the motorcycle?"

Since Mexico had a 100 percent tariff on all automobiles and motorcycles, people would drive motorcycles or cars down to Mexico and sell them to the locals for more than they were worth, which would still be less than what the locals would have paid.

"Where's the motorcycle? I gave it away."

Well, they weren't going to believe that shit. "No, you *sold* it to someone. . . ."

Next thing I know, we're in fucking jail again. Now, once a week, someone from the Tourist Relations Office in Cancun came down to Chetumal, just to talk to all the various foreigners who'd recently been arrested, me included. I told him the whole story. He didn't believe it, of course, but I convinced him to at least check it out. So, he did. That bastard went to the campground Mazatlán, and the American dude was still there with the bike, weeks after I'd given it to him. They confiscated it and charged me with "alienating my vehicle." I'm sure that some police chief in Mazatlán is still riding that bike today. Anyway, they let us out.

We went into Belize, stayed there for a couple of days, and then made our way slowly back to the US border crossing point at Calexico.

When I crossed the line, I got out of the van and kissed the dirt in sheer relief. There had been a few close shaves in Mexico, believe me. Not just that, there is a massive difference between the United States and Mexico. Anyone who has crossed the border and instantly seen the massive poverty and deprivation that is cut clean by an imaginary line called the national border knows that. However, I came back a totally new man.

ME: In what sense were you changed?

John McAfee: Before I went to Mexico, I'd looked at jobs as a means to earn money and to "get ahead." When I came back, getting ahead no longer mattered whatsoever. My profession was no longer a path to self-improvement. Fuck that. Now, I was looking at jobs as simply that go-to place where, whenever I ran out of money, I could show up for a few months or a year, get paid, and then continue doing what I was doing—*living.* And that's exactly what I have done ever since. Once I've filled my cup, why the fuck would I want to keep working? I turned the emphasis upside down.

ME: How do you think you were able to arrive at this place of enlightenment?

John McAfee: Charles Darwin. It's really that simple. He made me realize why I'm here. Obviously, we were just driving around Mexico in the van with no TV, etc. So in the evenings, it was a bit boring at these little campgrounds, and I became desperate for any English language book because, sadly, my Spanish just wasn't good enough for me to be entertained by reading a Spanish book. That would have been more like suffering. Somewhere I found a copy of Charles Darwin's *On the Origin of Species by Means of Natural Selection*, and thank God I was in Mexico when I found it because, had I been in the US, I'd have read three pages and put it down saying, "That's too heavy." But in Mexico, I had no fucking choice; it was all I had. I read that book from cover to cover—all 1,492 pages of very fine print.

ME: I'm not sure that I know anyone who has read it in its entirety?

John McAfee: Since 1975, when I read it, I've not met anyone else who has read it all, other than a college professor who taught evolution and therefore had to have read it. But that book changed my life in the sense that it instantly obviated the need for a divine presence in this universe. Not just that, in combination with my mathematical understanding of the universe, reading Darwin made me realize that the idea of a God was something I would never need. Now, I know that suggestion is blasphemous, especially in the eyes of fundamental Christians in America. Nevertheless, for me, it became the absolute truth.

ME: How much had you thought about religion since the Episcopal Church in Salem, Virginia?

John McAfee: Constantly. I have always questioned everything and trusted nobody—and that includes my own perception, which I can't always trust either. That is why I'm with Janice today, thirty-five years my younger and of sound sight and hearing. She is my eyes and ears nowadays. I need her to be that, for my own good.

More than anything, though, I'd always questioned what my place in the world was. What the fuck was I even here for? To me, that was essential to find out. Isn't that what everyone wants to know? I mean, aren't we're all just dumped on this planet with no fucking instruction manual?

Not just that, any instructions we did get are all oral and conflicting in the sense that the instructions relative to your parents differed from those related to your friends, which, in turn, conflicted with teachers, the police, and so on.

For me, there was no book that said, "OK, here you are. You are on Earth, which is a planet revolving around an unremarkable star in an ordinary galaxy at the edge of the universe. Now that you know your place, your situation is this: You are a living being, and you have been born with certain absolute qualities, which will develop throughout life. You may find, as you grow, that these qualities are contradictory. You might find yourself to be a loving, caring, generous, kind, and compassionate person. However, simultaneously, sometimes at the same second, you will find yourself to be hateful, angry, jealous, greedy, and lustful. So, now that you know the playing field, what do you do?"

All of these answers were missing for me until Darwin came into my life. When I speak about it, I feel like a Baptist minister inspired by the love of Christ. It answered every question I had ever had. It is the essence of living reality and how we are all, whether we like it or not, predator or prey. It was the right book at the right time in the right place.

ME: What, specifically, about Darwin's thinking resonated so much?

John McAfee: Darwin wasn't someone who just said, "Here's an idea. Maybe we came from apes...." No. He fleshed out every fucking thing. Even if someone was to say, "OK, great. But please tell me how a fucking eye can evolve?" They could go to Darwin, where there's an entire chapter on eyes. They'd read, get to the end, and then say, "Fuck, yes. I see."

Most people don't understand the brilliance of this man. He had the most underrated intelligence in modern history. But if you actually read the book, he subtly and smoothly explains the beauty of how we went from one-cell beings, energized by only light, to having eyeballs with a lens that can focus and receptors that can distinguish color, shape, and form. He illustrates how all of this could only have *evolved*. Darwin shows how there could have been no other way.

So in Mexico, I cried a lot as I read Darwin. Inevitably, Olivia thought I'd lost my fucking mind or was taking too many drugs. But it wasn't that at all. Instead, every page of Darwin revealed the answer to something that I'd previously troubled myself with. It was closure on a lot of years of questioning about my place in the world.

ME: How do you view religion and God nowadays?

John McAfee: I have barely even thought about religion in relation to myself since 1975. I have had no need to. But as far as religion itself is concerned generally, I now believe religion to simply be a construct of man.

If you think about it, it's all based on some kind of book, all of which was conceived and written by man, *about* a divine being. So we go to church with that book, and then we sing praises to Him on high. But all of that was created by the minds of men. On that basis, it makes no sense.

So, religion has got nothing to do with God in my mind. Religion is simply a matter of, "How do we pacify the people?" "How do we entertain people?" "How do we make people fear?" And the Christians, my friend, are the masters of that. In Christianity, you can frighten the people into doing almost anything by saying, "Listen, we have a strict set of rules. There is a narrow path you must walk, or else, you will be forever banned from heaven and paradise."

If that's not fear, I don't know what is. And at several points in history, fear has turned into absolute panic. Take the Spanish Inquisition, for instance. There's one of the prime examples of exactly how far religion can go.

ME: In what sense do you mean?

John McAfee: Well, it's not difficult to imagine church people sitting there thinking, "We're all kind of bored. There's not much happening in the world. But there's got to be bad people somewhere, right? Maybe there are witches. Or heretics. Or something. In fact, we *know* there are, so go and ferret those motherfuckers out and make sure that they cause us no more problem." That's religion for you.

ME: Should we separate religion from God on that basis?

John McAfee: God is a different question. And it's a question of you and your relationship to the world around you, as you understand it—all in an attempt to explain it all. On some level, that's what religion does:

explain things. But you didn't reach that conclusion through your own experience, through your own actions, or the pitfalls you fell into through improper actions.

No, God is something you have to create yourself—in your mind and in your perceptions. And you would only do that because you'd think, "This doesn't work for me without a God."

But equally, you don't have to create it at all. You might just say, "Fuck me, I think everything is perfect. I have no need for a God." That's me.

But until 1975, I had no idea that that choice even existed.

FIVE

POLIZEI!

It was February 2020, and our conversations had been going well. Rather than being the jagged, directionless pile of thoughts I had probably expected, to my surprise, McAfee had been refreshingly linear in his thinking. Not only that, but it also became obvious that he had enough self-awareness to recognize what the really key moments of his own life were, and he could present them in a way that made them relatable to anybody.

Also, it was becoming increasingly apparent that the man I was dealing with was anything but deranged and deluded—quite the reverse. I started looking forward to these conversations. In my line of work, co-writing, the primary aim has always got to be framing the story and getting it down. Sometimes I'm basically told, "Fuck off and come back in a year when you've written my book." That's fine. I'll do whatever it takes.

But for me, I'm always looking for an opportunity to learn something from the people I work with. If I'm not open to that possibility, what's the point of all this? It becomes just a job. An exciting one, sure, but a job nonetheless.

In this case, it felt like we were feeding off each other. Him the wise libertarian—me, the necessary vehicle required to tell his story.

And then, out of nowhere, he got sick.

I got a direct message on Skype to say that he was in bed, coughing and receiving oxygen. On the call a week prior, I had noticed he was coughing, but at the time, I thought nothing of it because he had often smoked a joint on these calls and the odd cough wasn't unusual. But now, he seemed really sick, and this was around the time that the first COVID-19 cases had started surfacing in some countries. Given that I never knew where he was, it was hard to tell if there was a possibility that he'd picked up the virus since not every country had recorded cases.

"Do you think you might have the coronavirus?" I asked.

"I don't know," he replied, "I should be out of bed in a few days."

With that, he sent a selfie of himself lying in a bed somewhere, looking really unwell and with an oxygen supply tube connected to his nose. He appeared to be at home, but medical help had clearly been called for.

I can't deny that I was concerned. The book at that moment didn't matter. I was more concerned about the man's health—not to mention that the whole idea of a global pandemic was only starting to gather pace at a serious level. By February of 2020, we'd moved past the "This might inconvenience us" stage to the "This will definitely paralyze the entire world for many months" phase of the COVID-19 pandemic.

Even when he resurfaced a week or so later, I'm not even sure if he knew what he'd had. Nobody was testing at that point; nobody really knew enough about the symptoms to make an assessment. McAfee certainly had his views on the virus, even at that stage,

"It's a biological trial, no doubt about it," he said.

Then he just kept typing while I stared at the screen....

Here is the thing

Forget Corona virus

Forget everything

This will be the book of the century

This I know

Better than I know my own name

Believe me on this, if you believe nothing else

This I know

Without ego

Or any self-involvement

Of any kind

Act appropriately

For some reason

Both of us have lucked out

Do not fuck this up

You have the world's biggest tiger by the tail

Your problem now

Not mine ☺

When it all shifts to mine, I will bear my weight

I suspect that together we can change the world

Even a tiny amount might help.

Call me when you are ready to talk again

I had, of course, no idea what any of this meant. Was he high on pain meds or high on something else? I knew he had re-established an affinity with drugs in recent years, and he'd alluded to their use without ever discussing them in detail. But, on the other hand, I'd seen these odd stream-of-consciousness-type lists before in our earliest email communications. However, this one had been unprompted, and I had no idea how to reply. So I didn't, other than sending a solitary thumbs up emoji, which in retrospect looked a bit insulting in its brevity relative to his diatribe.

Nevertheless, a week later, when I felt sure he'd be well enough to talk, I scrolled to the last entry on his list, opened Skype, and pressed "call."

JOHN MCAFEE: After leaving Mexico, Olivia and I went back to Cincinnati. Why? We had friends there, and quite frankly, we had nowhere else to go. We had some cash, in addition to some of the serious shit we scored in Mexico, which included some ancient Mayan artifacts, which we later found out we'd taken out of Mexico illegally. Suffice to say, I offloaded that shit pretty quickly. We then rented a tiny apartment. However, Mexico had been a serious out-of-country experience. Other than a week in London when I was sixteen, where I'd met a few cute English girls, learned some British slang, and developed enough of an accent to sound somewhat cool when I returned to high school, I'd never really had any out-of-country experience that I could relate to. Mexico changed my worldview.

ME: What about when you worked for Xerox in London?

JOHN MCAFEE: Xerox didn't really qualify. I was in London during the week, but I wasn't *immersed* in the culture, simply because I was getting on a flight every Friday afternoon and coming back to Rochester. I had a foot in two places. That, for me, is something completely different from entirely submitting to another culture, as Olivia and I had done for a full year in Mexico.

From this point on, I was only interested in working overseas, and it wasn't long before I landed a job working for Computer Sciences Corporation in Munich, Germany, on what was meant to be a two-year-long contract with Siemens, Germany's largest electrical manufacturer, who had just purchased RCA's worldwide computer division. Everybody was trying to get ahead in computers, but few were succeeding.

My specific role was to oversee the integration of RCA into Siemens, a piece of cake for me at that point. By this time, it felt as if the technology was part of my hands, simply an extension of me. I didn't have to think about it; my brain just did it. I was now on a different trajectory.

ME: What do you mean by a different trajectory?

John McAfee: My only goal now was to do as little actual work as possible and to experience as much of the world as I could at the same time. How did I do it? Well, here's how.

At Siemens, I spent a few days at the company and quickly realized two things. First, I saw how woefully inadequate the whole operation was. Second, I realized that the whole culture of this job just wasn't going to work for me. But I didn't tell them that, of course. They'd have just fired me and found someone else.

So what I did was what I do best: used my laziness, aka my mathematics, and computer knowledge to create a company architecture plan in a matter of days that fucking blew them away. They said, "How did you manage to do all this in less than a week?" "Oh, I've been working on this before I even started officially," I told them—the aim being to further ingratiate myself by suggesting that I'd been working prior to even being paid.

ME: What was the aim of this approach?

John McAfee: I was learning that if I demonstrated extreme competence right off the bat, which I always could, I could do what the fuck I wanted thereafter. "Now that you've seen that I'm competent," I said, "let me explain something. I need you to understand how serious this is. It is impossible for me to do my best work in an office environment. I can do it, but you're not going to get this level of creativity. And you're not going to get this level of output. So I am going to work from home.

If you need me in the office for a meeting on a Friday, I'd be more than happy to come in to give you an update."

ME: And they bought this shit?

JOHN MCAFEE: Of course. Not only that, but the work that I took into the meetings on a Friday was stuff I whipped together in half an hour! I just walked in and threw it on the goddamn table. It might have taken someone else a week, but not me.

I had the entire two-year project done in the first month I was there. It was stored away in my dresser in pieces that I could have delivered immediately. But I didn't. I dripped it out once a week, knowing that I could get fucked up beyond belief to the point that I couldn't speak, but still, if I could dress myself, shave and get to the office every Friday for an hour, I could show that I'd done my work for the week.

ME: So you got fucked up for the other six and a half days of the week?

JOHN MCAFEE: Well...during that time, I integrated myself into the busking community. You are European. You know what that word means, right?

ME: You mean street musicians?

John McAfee: Exactly. Street musicians. We don't have the word "buskers" in the United States. It started when I befriended a man called Phil Free, who was an older guy even back then. He is dead now, and there was a video online of his funeral, and everybody at it I knew, even though I hadn't spoken to or seen any of them for thirty years. You can probably find that and other information about him on YouTube.

Anyway, what happened is that all these buskers started living with me in this two-bedroomed flat I had behind the Hofbräuhaus on Hernnstrasse. There were maybe thirty people residing with me at one point, most of them sleeping on mattresses on various floors spaces. I had my own mattress on the floor in my bedroom; others slept in my room also. Various women would come and go; sometimes Phil would sleep with me and one or two women. As you can probably imagine, it turned into a very shady existence indeed.

ME: What did you want from this type of unorthodox living arrangement?

John McAfee: I didn't want anything. I have never really wanted anything. I was just *living* and meeting people that were fascinating to me. I started painting at the time. I'd stay up all night partying if I felt like it. Or I'd sleep all day. Or maybe we'd go to Switzerland for three days—leave on a Tuesday and come back on a Thursday. Technically, I was meant to be working. But I didn't have to call my work or ask anyone for permission to do anything. There were no plans or goals. I was living a free-form existence—that's all that this was. All you need to live that kind of life is money, and they were paying me more of it than I could spend.

ME: How long did this permission-less existence continue for?

John McAfee: It all came to an end, and in not the best of circumstances. After a year and a half, my girlfriend Olivia left because I was having an affair.

I'm a womanizer and don't deny it. I cannot be faithful and never have been to anyone. Of course, I have *promised* fidelity to a number of live-in girlfriends at various times, but never, at any time have I honored that promise. Inevitably, women left me because of other women. And if they didn't leave me, I left them, never because of another woman, but instantly another woman would show up nevertheless. That is how my life has always been.

So in Munich, I was having an affair with the boss's secretary. Simultaneously, I was having an affair with pretty much every waitress at the Hofbräuhaus, and thirty buskers were living in my flat. It was tumultuous. Olivia had just had enough.

ME: So what happened with the flat and the buskers?

John McAfee: One night, one of the buskers brings in this sketchy dude and a girl that looked like she could have been twenty. I suppose she could also have been much younger. Anyway, this guy turned out to be really crazy. He was abusive to the girl, was yelling at her, etc. I didn't know if he was on drugs or whether was just a sick dude. Either way, two of the buskers forcefully booted him out, literally dragged his ass down the stairs (my place was on the second floor) and threw him out into the street. Man, he was pissed.

We went back to doing what we were doing: smoking, listening to loud music, drinking, and then, a couple of hours later the intercom buzzer went—"Polizei!"

Now, everyone in the apartment heard this, and so I replied, "Give me a moment," to buy a little time. While I said this, it seemed like chaos was ensuing behind me. But it wasn't chaos. No, it was the beginning of order.

By the time the police and this dude we'd just thrown out reached the second floor, the flat had been transformed. From being scattered around, smoking weed and drinking, suddenly everyone was standing, chatting informally to each other quietly in gentile poses in one room. The jazz-rock music that we'd been playing had been turned down and replaced with quiet classical. Meanwhile, Phil and Anton, a violin player from Spain, were playing a quiet game of chess in another room. We had never even played chess before. I don't even know how they knew where the fucking chess set was! Basically, despite the lingering aroma of weed, the flat was a picture of civil serenity.

ME: What did the police make of all this?

John McAfee: Well, these friends of mine weren't stupid. They put two and two together very quickly. A dude had been booted out; half an hour later, the police showed up. So they had already taken the young girl up to the fourth floor and one of them, another girl called Marianne, sat with her on the landing while the police were giving the flat a look over.

But I could tell that the police still weren't quite sure about everything. "What kind of a place is this?" one of them asked, while peering over my shoulder at the confusing but simultaneously disarming scene behind me. "These are just a few friends of mine," I told them. "Where's the girl?" they asked. "She left," I said.

In the absence of a reason to do anything by way of enforcing a law, the police were about to leave, or at least they were until the asshole we'd just thrown out reached into his pocket and pulled out a lump of hash, which he handed to one of the policemen and said, "They gave me this. They gave me this!"

Well fuck me, I thought.

One policeman looked at the other, and then, rather than arresting anyone, he just said, "zu klein" the German equivalent of "It's too small" to his colleague. They shrugged in unison, put the lump down on the hall table, and walked out. There was no fucking way they were going to arrest twenty-five people for a tiny amount of hashish. We'd dodged a bullet. It was a miracle.

ME: So you got away with it. What was the problem?

John McAfee: We did, but even still, I sensed a distant ill wind. To me, that whole incident felt like the beginning of the end, and that sense was only confirmed when, having brought the girl down late that night, she confessed to us that next morning that she was actually only sixteen and not twenty, by which point she had already had sex with Phil.

Now, I have always had a very good sense of impending doom. And I also know that when you push something too far, it always, always breaks. In Germany, I had pushed everything to the limit and beyond: my job, drugs, drink, morals…everything. Something was going to break.

ME: Did you want to cut your losses?

John McAfee: Yes, exactly. I reviewed the whole situation. On one hand, I'd done almost no work, perhaps a sum total of eight hours in two years, and had been paid a quarter of a million dollars for doing so. But on the other, Olivia had long gone, and I knew that my name was on that fucking flat door—a flat to where the police had shown up and there had been an underage girl, albeit they never physically saw her there. And then I also figured that the crazy dude we'd kicked out wasn't the type of guy who seemed like he'd let things go very easily. All the warnings were there.

I cleared out of the flat the very next morning. I didn't have much in the way of possessions, but I did have quite a nice Marantz audio system with all the bells and whistles, which I knew that my upstairs neighbor had always admired. So I sold it to him for $1,000—a third of what it was probably worth—and got on a flight to London, from where I called my boss in Germany and told him that I was resigning. It was the day that Elvis Presley died—August 16, 1977. That was the last time I ever set foot in Germany.

ME: Had you missed America?

John McAfee: As fantastic an out-of-country experience as Germany had been, yes, I had. I'd reached a point after two years where I just wanted a McDonald's burger and to go and visit some past girlfriends who were either scintillating conversationalists or great fucks. So I found myself back in New York in August of 1977, looking for another job that would let me continue living this itinerant life.

ME: Did you want to get straight back into another job?

John McAfee: At this point, again, I could have had pretty much any job I wanted in my field. I'd worked with NASA and Univac, and had knowledge of all areas of operating systems and process automation. I was a dynamic computer architect that everybody knew about. The technology world also knew that, if I designed something, it was going to be current, innate, and fascinating.

In the end, I chose a job at Booz Allen Hamilton, just like Edward Snowden later did. And the reason I chose them was that it was a consulting house that was in all likelihood going to send me away—to God knows where—after an initial training period in New York City. That whole idea appealed to me, as much as I liked being back in the US temporarily.

At the same time, I called up an ex-girlfriend, Joyce, who I'd met when I was in Rochester. I'd been fucking her, along with several others, while I was married, when I was working for Xerox. I told her to come and live with me in New York, and she did. I spent the next month in intensive training.

ME: Given your level of expertise at that time, was there anything left to train you in?

John McAfee: As I said, being a management consultancy, Booz Allen was a different kind of company from all the others I'd worked at. And their training program was every bit as valuable to me as those summer months at General Electric had been years prior. Instead of mastering process automation, at Booz Allen, I learned how to write high-level corporate proposals. It was a solid month of fucking work, and I'm glad I went through it.

Then they sent me to Texas to work on a job at the National Bank of Texas in Dallas. It was only a two-month job; I did it, went back to New York, and was only there for about three weeks before they said, "Does anybody here speak Portuguese?" Nobody raised a hand. And so, I did.

ME: Did you speak any Portuguese?

John McAfee: Fuck no! But my thinking was that, having been in Mexico for that year, my Spanish was tolerable. Then I assumed that because Spanish and Portuguese were so similar, that I'd probably be able to figure it out. Regardless, they sent me to Rio de Janeiro to work on a job with the Brazilian phone company, Embratel. I was to be the manager of development for their new telephone switching system. As the manager, I knew I'd be able to do whatever the fuck I wanted. As such, I viewed this assignment as either the best thing or the worst thing that was ever going to happen to me.

ME: What sort of outlook did you go down to South America with?

JOHN MCAFEE: I was still very much in that mode where any job I did was simply to fund my lifestyle. And I wanted to achieve that by doing as little work as was humanly possible. And, from that perspective, Embratel had two problems right off the bat.

Firstly, I did not speak the language. However, everybody spoke English. So, right up front, when I introduced myself to my team, I laid out the ground rules: "The reason that you are having problems is that you are behind the Americans, behind the Germans—behind the developed world. And the reason you are behind the developed world is because of language. English is the international of business. And it is also the international language of technology. So, while I'm here, we will all speak nothing but English." Anytime anyone came to me babbling anything in Portuguese, I just held my hand up and said, "English, please." Problem solved.

The second problem they had was that I had no intention of being in the office often enough to fucking care whether anyone was speaking English or not. How did I pull that off? Well, I pulled the same shit I pulled at Siemens and have pulled many times since. And it works every fucking time.

ME: I see a theme here. You've got to deliver the goods early, right?

JOHN MCAFEE: Exactly. You must be able to prove your worth by delivering *something*. That's what I always did. So during the first week, I delivered a complete proposal: how we were going to do everything, detailed timeframes—it was fucking perfect both technically and from a business perspective, and I then explained to them why it was: "Now, I'd like to explain that I developed this proposal before I even came down here. I think that you will find that this is the best possible proposal imaginable and that I am the man to carry this out and make sure it is implemented to the letter."

ME: I feel like a 'but' is coming?

John McAfee: "But…I cannot work in an office environment with other people: noises, voices, doors being closed, and footsteps going by. I regret to tell you that I am severely handicapped in such an environment. Therefore, I simply have to work from home in order to be able to implement the proposal I've just shown you. And, indeed, I am perfectly willing to come in anytime you really need me, and perhaps may I suggest once a week on a Friday, to show you what I've done that week. If at any time you feel that what I have done is insufficient, then I swear to you that I'll come in to this office twenty-four hours a day." "OK, that sounds good," they said. Two problems solved.

ME: I'm imagining Booz Allen looked after their consultants overseas?

John McAfee: Again, within the first week I had the whole project done. This time it was on a bookshelf in my expensive condo, instead of in a dresser in a flat I shared with thirty vagrants. Once again, I didn't have to do any work. I didn't have a care in the world.

Well now, Germany was one thing, but now here I was in fucking Rio de Janeiro—another proposition altogether—with a condo and a full-time maid, while getting paid $300,000 a year in addition to having every conceivable expense covered on top of that. What do you think fucking happened?

Well, the first thing that happened was that the girl, in this case, Joyce, went home—as all girls who were with me always did. And she did this because, as usual, I simply couldn't be faithful. It just wasn't in me. I was never rude about it. It wasn't like I ever came home and said, "Joyce, I have a new girlfriend, so why don't you sleep on the sofa?"

No, I was always polite, but she left nevertheless, leaving me in Rio alone with a job I don't have to go to. Shit. I must admit that life became a little unraveled, as it always did when I had too much money and time on my hands.

ME: Rio is a place of great contrasts, yes? Wealth and poverty being the first juxtaposition that springs to mind.

John McAfee: Yes, but before I tell you about it, can I just say that all of this is very good for me.

ME: What are you referring to? This conversation?

John McAfee: Not specifically this one, but all of this. I have never told my life story before because I have never had a need to. Furthermore, who the fuck wants to listen to all this shit anyway?

ME: Well, I suspect a lot of people might. In the meantime, can you give me a sense of what living in Rio was like?

John McAfee: Let me give you a sense of my existence, and before I do, let me tell you that all the women in Rio are like Greek goddesses. That would be fine if it wasn't for the fact that all the men are like Greek gods. You've got them to compete with, and the only way to do so was by playing on the fact that you are an American with a lot of money. Consequently, my relationship with women changed somewhat in Brazil in the sense that now I had to shine a lot on those features about myself that would make these women want to fuck me rather than the Greek god beside me at the bar.

ME: Are you saying that you consciously changed your approach to meeting women?

John McAfee: I had no choice but to accentuate what I had: that I was a wealthy American. And I did that by dressing American, spending freely, and taking women back to my fancy condominium, where I had the maid wait on them hand and foot, etc. Then and only then would I succeed in getting these women into bed.

ME: I'd like to know more about what moved you, though. Or what motivated you. Or what interested you.

John McAfee: I didn't think that had anything to do with this book.

ME: I think it's got everything to do with this book. I want to know the real you.

John McAfee: Well, OK. Now, the Brazilian people—at least in the Rio area—are called Cariocas, a mix of Portuguese and native, and let me tell you, that that's a beautiful mix. Not just that, but they also have rituals that are way different from any Christian rituals you might see in America or beyond.

Every morning, I used to go to the beach just as the sun was rising. One day when I got there, there was this bunch of women milling around maybe three hundred yards down the beach in one direction. In the other direction, a similar distance away, was this whole group of men, from which some kind of rhythmic music—drumming, etc.—was emanating. Suddenly, this singing started, this longing, wailing sound, and it was the women. The sound they were making was hard to describe, but it was as if there was an emptiness that needed to be filled. The men responded with a song that sounded not as if they were empty, but that they were full and on fire.

These groups moved toward each other, dancing, until suddenly there was this melee of flailing arms and legs. There was nobody actually copulating as far as I saw, but they could well have been while standing up.

ME: How did this mating ritual make you feel?

John McAfee: It was a dance of such overwhelming sexual power; I was just stunned. You asked me what moved me or motivated me. Well, watching these people did. They must have thought I was stupid; I just stood there with my mouth wide open. Apparently, this ceremony preceded Carnival every year. And when Carnival started, everything shut down in Rio, including my work office, not that I noticed given that I was never actually in the office.

ME: Did you throw yourself into the Carnival spirit?

John McAfee: I didn't have any choice. Everything closed. I couldn't buy bread—nothing. So I found myself wandering the streets of Ipanema, the little beach suburb where my condo was. I remember standing there in the street, hearing the revelers approaching. In the distance, I could see that they were filling the entire width of the thoroughfare like a wave. As they approached me, it was as if an arm, a welcoming arm comprised of many people, reached out and pulled me in. The next thing I knew I was in the carnival and engulfed by the feeling of unconditional love that came with it.

ME: How did that feel?

John McAfee: It's so hard to describe, but I could definitely feel it. I was part of something where there were no barriers and no judgment. I have never experienced anything like it in my life. Four days later, I had slept with more women than I could possibly count and in the most natural possible way. I remember being with this girl. She was hot, and we had already slept together.

Then she met a boy, whereupon she turned to me and said something to the effect of, "You have been so much fun. But I want to sleep with this man now." So she brought this dude over, and the two of them then decided how to replace the girl for me. "You would really like Antonia. And I think I saw her. Wait here. You're going to love her." And Antonia came, and I did love her. We went off, and the other couple went off somewhere else.

ME: It sounds as if there something about the openness that resonated with you?

John McAfee: That, my friend, was the actualization of freedom. I have never since seen a better example of how to handle something as inherently natural as sexual relations. I can't remember feeling more respected and more part of something than when this girl I'd just slept with told me she wanted to sleep with someone else, in the most loving and accepting of ways. There is just no bullshit in Carnival. It is just too full of itself. It is reality. There is no room for negativity in there. I left Brazil when the job finished. Again, I was enlightened more by my experiences of life than any work I'd actually done.

However, living in Rio and seeing what super-rich people do with yachts and what have you made me think, *I've never experienced that. Is there a way to become super-rich without ever actually working?*

ME: And is there?

John McAfee: No, there is none. I could have continued doing what I was doing, which by anyone's standards was quite extreme, and been moderately rich. But I wasn't going to get super-rich doing what I'd been doing for the previous five years—phoning my boss and telling him I was going to work from home, etc.

I returned to New York City and given that I'd done two good jobs, I was given a bit more of a heads up about what jobs were available. One of them was a contract with Blue Cross Blue Shield in New York City, so I thought, *Fuck me, I just got back from the most exotic place on the planet, I'm totally down with being in New York City for a while.*

ME: What was the nature of this job?

John McAfee: Blue Cross Blue Shield was the largest health insurance company in America at the time. I didn't go there because of the nature of their business; I went there because they were expanding tremendously and needed to beef up their programming staff by hundreds.

As the manager of programming, one of my jobs was to increase the programming staff. At the time, they were going through an employment agency, paying them three or four thousand dollars each for every employee. Obviously, this amounted to millions of dollars in the long run, so the first thing I thought was, *I don't need those fucks.* And from there, I started my own consulting house with the help of a young lawyer I'd met at a singles bar, for the sole purpose of being able to hire staff for myself.

ME: I have to say that this all sounds highly dubious....

John McAfee: I don't think this young lawyer was ever totally clear about what I was doing. But since I was the manager of programming, I already knew most of the good programmers in the world at that point. Most of them had worked with or for me somewhere at some stage or another. At Siemens, I'd had sixty of the best. At Embratel, I'd had over a hundred. I knew exactly who to hire, so I just called people up and said, "Do you want a great job? Why don't you come to New York and work at Blue Cross Blue Shield?" Those who said yes, I then told them to call the young lawyer to formalize it all, and he'd then refer back to me through my secretary, so I had their records, etc. Instead of the employment agency getting fees for these new hires, my consulting house did.

ME: Obviously this was all highly illegal, and I'm assuming this scam got found out?

John McAfee: The biggest tragedy of all of this was that I had persuaded many friends to come to New York to work for Blue Cross Blue Shield, and to simultaneously fill the bank account of my consulting house to near bursting point. I made millions, until one day my boss—not my Blue Cross Blue Shield boss but my Booz Allen Hamilton boss—walked into my office. I had a recorder sitting on my desk, and I knew I was in serious trouble when he pointed to it and said, "Is that on?" "No," I told him.

ME: He'd figured out what you were doing?

John McAfee: Yes, he had, and I never found out how he did. What I'd been doing wasn't technically a criminal offense for which I could be punished from a legal perspective, but it was a serious conflict of interest for which people could get fired, which I did. Given that all the money was coming into my consulting house from Blue Cross Blue Shield, my being fired essentially killed off that consulting house right there and then. I certainly wasn't going to start a *real* employment agency, knocking on doors offering people jobs. Unfortunately, all the people I'd brought to New York City to be part of this scheme were also let go.

ME: Do you regret involving these innocent people in this hustle?

John McAfee: On one hand, I suppose I regret bringing them. But the thing about me is that—and I'm being truthful—I am blissful where I am right now. And I know that if I changed anything about my life, even the tiniest thing, I wouldn't be here right now at all. So as tricky as it is, from that perspective, I guess I would do it all again. Unfortunately, we don't have that choice. We don't get do-overs, so it's all hypothetical nonsense. But that was the last time I ever attempted to make money via those means.

ME: What happened next?

John McAfee: In the midst of all of this, while I was working at Blue Cross Blue Shield, I had fallen in love with one of my employees—a lady called Claire—and subsequently married her.

SIX

DUALITY

McAfee spent a lot of his time talking about women. Indeed, he had had more women in his life than perhaps anyone I've ever known, and to that extent, it was easy enough to imagine that some of the internet rumors that suggested he'd fathered over thirty children in his life, could well be true.

I wanted to talk to him about women some more, and his relationship with them over the adult years, but before I did, he started the next call telling me that he was late because he'd just got off the phone with, coincidentally, a woman, Deanna Lorraine, a former YouTube host and relationship coach, who also happened to be running as a Republican congresswoman in California's twelfth district.

As much as I always wanted to keep McAfee on track, sometimes it was simply impossible. In any case, I'd come to realize that some of his most insightful thinking came not just when I prompted him, but also when he just felt like it. To that end, when these detours arose, I more than often let him run.

ME: Why did this politician call you?

JOHN MCAFEE: She wanted to know if she could use my name privately as one of her supporters. So I said yes because I don't give a shit who I endorse. If somebody wants to say, "John McAfee is a supporter of mine," why would I care?

Not long ago, I also contacted Andrew Yang and told him that I'd like to throw my support behind him for the presidential campaign. I plan to do the same thing with everyone, because why not? And then I thought: *If I'm doing this for presidential candidates, why not also for congressmen or women*? I, a presidential candidate myself, am happy to throw my weight behind Deanna.... I can't remember her surname.

ME: Deanna Lorraine is her name, and some would say that she has some controversial views.

John McAfee: Her name doesn't really matter because, generally speaking, none of these people matter. I don't give a shit about her views either, good God.

ME: What do you mean?

John McAfee: In my mind, they might as well be automatons. In fact, they *are* automatons—to the extent that you can predict exactly what they are going to say and do. They are like computer programs in the sense that if you input certain commands, you will get the same responses every time. Therefore, it does not matter who sits on a chair in any official office. In America, that chair has essentially been a vacant office since the late 1950s anyway. They might as well grab some random street vermin who doesn't speak or write and put him in that goddamn chair for four years. It wouldn't make any difference.

ME: I take it you are cynical about politicians/presidents generally? Isn't that ironic given you've tried to be one?

John McAfee: Let's call it what it is. That chair has been occupied by a set of profoundly charismatic and articulate actors that have all simply pretended that they play on the same team as the rest of us poor schmucks.

ME: Does that sentiment not apply to every politician anywhere?

John McAfee: I don't want to come over as being cynical about every aspect of life, so what about Mahatma Gandhi as the exception? Can we talk about him for a second? What part of anything he ever did was self-serving? But that's the only one I know. Of course, there is a possibility that he too was merely a shadow created by the media. But there were also too many eyewitness accounts of his actions in the role of a servant—whatever company he was in—for that mirage to be the case. If that was acting, then, fuck me, that was an interesting play and one that I'd like to watch. If it wasn't, then the man just loved people and life, and he just wanted people and life to be better so that the world in which he lived would become a better place. I would elect a million of those men long before I'd elect anyone who pays a hundred million dollars to land a goddamn job.

ME: But technically, you fall into that latter category. How do you square that away?

John McAfee: As I've told you, I'm not going to be president, and nobody is going to elect me to anything. I'm just making a point that anybody can do it.

ME: Before we continue with the story, I want to talk to you about women again generally because it's such a big part of your life, and I have to confess to not really understanding your motivations on that front. Also, you've just told me, out of the blue, that you got married—while at the same time telling me that you can't be faithful.

John McAfee: My life with women always followed a certain pattern. As I told you, Alexa was my first great love when I was a teenager. Then, our paths kept crossing thereafter. And then from her, the first time I went to a woman called Karen when I was a freshman in college. She was older than me, more experienced sexually than me, and I liked that. While I was with her, everyone else was excluded. Where my apartment near the campus would normally be full of people, booze, and women, that all changed while I was with Karen. Eventually, I got tired of Karen, and then all my friends came back, and it was a free-for-all for a while until I found someone new.

ME: When you say it was a free-for-all, how did that play out practically?

John McAfee: I might have had one new woman every day in five. Then I might have had fifteen in one weekend. It wasn't as if it was a contest or anything; I just loved women and had since that first kiss in the woods. I have often described taking heroin as like being kissed by God. But that's not the case. Truly being kissed by God is when circumstances occur that you just couldn't predict the outcome.

Like when I kissed that young girl in the woods I told you about, I didn't know if she'd run away, or scream, or hit me. She saw me coming, but she didn't run away. She was just waiting—for what, she didn't know. And when it was over, she never ever mentioned the incident to anyone, not even me. I hardly remember seeing her after that even though she must have still been in my class for the remainder of that year.

But my point is that, after that experience, that adventure, I must have thought, *What do I need you for?* She was just an innocent victim in a monumental moment in someone else's life. A twisted moment of molestation provided a moment of enlightenment for John McAfee, and regardless of what people might think of that, I will not back away from that.

ME: Are you being serious when you call this molestation? You were seven.

John McAfee: Are you kidding? In today's America, it would be. Someone, probably both of us, would be in therapy. We are the font of political correctness. We are the shining banner for the faithful sheep. They are not going to like what I just said. But I want you to say it anyway.

ME: OK, I feel like we're getting somewhere with this. Are you then saying that all of your relationships with women over the years have simply been an attempt to recapture this feeling, and not about the women themselves?

John McAfee: I don't think I was chasing the feeling, but I do think I've been chasing that doorway all my life to a degree, via a multitude of different women. Of course, at some point, I realized that I didn't actually need the women, but even then, my habituated body would still say, "Well, if there's nothing else happening, I want sex." And for me, that was never much work. I could call someone to come over, go to a whorehouse or a bar. I could always find sex and excitement.

ME: All of this makes relationships, like the marriage you just told me you entered into in 1980 with Claire, almost impossible, right?

John McAfee: Oh, yes. How could I ever have success in a marriage? The problem is, I have lived two lives regarding women throughout my life: when a special woman was there, and when a special woman wasn't there. In each instance, I was two completely different people. When there was no special woman there, I was in bachelor mode and did exactly as I wanted, mostly driven by physical impulses that inevitably led, given I am a sex addict, to frequent sexual encounters. My mind, the part that says, "Dude, why are you even doing this?" was completely disengaged.

When that special woman was there, I was truly attempting to be the proper person that deserved that woman's attention. And to do that, I tried to truly understand that woman's needs—the most notable need usually being that I wouldn't go down the street and fuck somebody else. If I had to be faithful, I would absolutely do my best. During these times, I truly wanted to know these women and, specifically, why it was that I was with them in the first place. There had to be a fucking reason, and I always wanted to know what that reason was.

ME: Did you find these reasons?

John McAfee: Of course not. If you think you consciously know why you do shit, then I doubt you're the same species as me. If you sit and analyze the sequences of events, you'll realize that your conscious thoughts play such a tiny role in why things happen, that you might as well discount them completely. Why? Because there's a big fucking world out there, with its own ideas and its own chaotic direction. We're just thrown in the middle of all that shit, and if we think that chaos gives a shit about any individual member of that pool of chaos, well it doesn't.

ME: Are you suggesting that we don't really choose anything in life including wives?

John McAfee: Do you really think I chose to be here: on the run, with a woman thirty-five years younger than me, who was an ex-prostitute who has also tried to kill me? I didn't, but I am here, and we are happy and married on paper. Chaos brought us here. Chaos, of some kind or another, brought me into every relationship and every marriage I was ever in.

ME: Based on everything that you've told me, why do you keep getting married?

John McAfee: As I've alluded to already, I am basically two people. One part of me wants to conform, not to people, but to the accepted norms of the world, just so that I don't run around hurting and offending people just by being me. That's one part, the part where I say to myself, "Jesus, dude, you can't do this. People are going to get hurt."

Then the other part of me says, "Yeah, but I'm sorry. I am just not happy living like that," and that extends into every aspect of my life: health, spirituality, sex, relationships, and work. I have been at war with me forever.

So, the person that keeps getting married is that one who simply doesn't want to make any waves, right? The dude that just wants to get through a day without going to jail, being shot at, or having a woman hold a knife at my throat, which has happened more than once. The other person is the one who sees an attractive woman and says, "Good God. I am aroused." And then what do I do? Naturally, I try to get her into bed. I do not know how to stop that impulse or even why I should.

ME: Which person is the real you?

John McAfee. Both are. That's the point.

ME: I think you're more self-aware than most and, to that extent, very open about your faults.

John McAfee: That may be. But the thing I learned long ago is that, as much as we might want to, we cannot hide who we really are. It comes out in your actions, your words, the shifting of your eyes, and your daily choices. Please God, you can't hide shit. That can't be hidden. Can I ask you a question?

ME: Of course.

John McAfee: Do you think there's a book here? The reason that I'm working with you is that you are mature enough and experienced enough to understand my life. You are a mirror for me. I am using you.

ME: Why do you feel the need to ask?

John McAfee: Well, I don't want to do something worthless that wouldn't interest anyone. I want a real book, where people can actually learn something from my life. If we can do that, I'll be very happy.

ME: My turn to ask a question: do you have in the region of forty-seven children as has been said in the press?

John McAfee: That's a whole story in itself. I have five that I know about, but I have no way of knowing the number for sure. However, what I do know is that literally dozens of women have inevitably come out of the woodwork over the years, claiming that I was the father of their child. That, however, does not mean that I am. Of this number, a percentage I had never even met. They could be eliminated immediately. Of the remainder, a proportion of those I'd never had sex with. They too could be discounted. Then there was a bunch of women who I may have had sex with, but the age of the child relative to when we'd last seen each other made it impossible for me to have been the father. But the rest? Pure conjecture.

ME: Let's go back. It's 1981. The boss at Booz Allen Hamilton has just fired you for a serious conflict of interest, and you've just married Claire. What next?

JOHN MCAFEE: We decided to try our luck and head to California. We went to Palo Alto, the center of Silicon Valley, got an apartment, and Claire started working for a well-known computer technology company.

Meanwhile, I got a job working for a company called Four-Phase Systems, which built smart data entry terminals back then. They wanted me to develop operating systems for them, and I did what I had always done: turned up rarely, did a great job, but within months, I got bored senseless and left.

Shortly afterward, I took another job with another Silicon Valley company called Omex, which was the first company making optical memory, which facilitated, at least for those days, far greater memory capability than magnetic memory. We were barely at the beginning of the technology age.

ME: From a historical perspective, how did Silicon Valley happen?

JOHN MCAFEE: Its origins by far pre-dated me showing up there in 1982, let's put it that way. From my understanding, it just organically happened. San Francisco was always a mecca for the drug scene, which most techies have always belonged to, probably because of Stanford University's status as a draw for research into computer sciences dating back to the late 1960s. Then that synergy of all those techies being attracted to San Francisco probably just created a spontaneous technological revolution.

From there, expansion South, along El Camino Real—the street continuing fifty miles from San Francisco to San Jose as it does today—was inevitable. In 1983, it was probably twenty miles long and five miles wide. There were car companies, service industries, and technology. That's all there was in Silicon Valley.

ME: What happened at Omex?

John McAfee: On one hand, the work at Omex was some of the most technically challenging work I'd ever done. I was the director of software engineering for the company, and unlike most of my other jobs, I was in the office almost all the time. The problem was, even though my colleague, the director of hardware, was the straightest motherfucker on the planet in that he didn't smoke, drink, or take drugs, the wider culture at Omex was completely hedonistic, to the extent that people, me included, were literally snorting coke off their desks and, me included, having group sex in the conference room. It was here, at Omex, that my drug consumption reached an all-time high. I was absolutely out of control. One of my life's great turning points was looming on the horizon.

ME: What drugs were you taking?

John McAfee: Let's see. Psychedelics, mushrooms, cocaine, speed, marijuana—whatever I could get my hands on at the time. Inevitably, my wife and I separated, and she is still in Silicon Valley now working, though I haven't talked to her for many, many years.

ME: Why did you separate?

John McAfee: The usual reasons. I couldn't stay faithful. At first, I went from my wife, Claire, to another girlfriend briefly, and then ultimately to the woman who would end up being my third wife, Linda.

I met Linda while I was still at Omex, and I did so because one of our suppliers at the time was located in New Jersey. Consequently, every now and then, I'd have to fly over to New Jersey for business meetings and to resolve technical issues, and, on one occasion when I was flying back, I was getting ready to board the plane in Newark.

In those days, I was into motorcycles, so I got into the habit of wearing cowboy boots because they prevented your calves from getting burned on the bike exhaust. Anyway, I was with this colleague of mine, Jeff, a crazy motherfucker who also happened to be a brilliant computer mind. We had dropped acid, or some other psychedelic, and just as the airline representative was saying, "Mr. McAfee, we need to leave, can you please board the plane," I stood up and had this sudden sensation that, for the first time in my entire life, one of my legs was shorter than the other. It wasn't just a little shorter; there was a significant difference. I said to myself, "How on Earth have I never noticed this?" I started taking my boots off because I just had to see this for myself. "Mr. McAfee, we have to leave," the woman working for the airline said again. "But one of my legs is shorter than the other!" I kept saying.

That woman was Linda. She was so sweet, even though I was clearly out of my mind on acid. Once I finally got on the plane, she gave me a nice quiet seat up the back and then came and sat with me. By the end of the flight, I just had to ask her out. Next thing I know, we're getting married and living together in Santa Clara. The only problem was that I never actually divorced Claire.

ME: Obviously that was illegal, yes?

JOHN MCAFEE: This will be the first time any of this has been revealed. I have never discussed any of this before, but, at this point, I don't mind it being out there. In my eyes, it was so long ago that the legal aspect of it doesn't really matter. I just never got around to divorcing Claire, and, in any case, she somehow went off and married someone else, so I guess it didn't really matter. Anyway, I married Linda. We would be together for seventeen years thereafter.

ME: How were things at home at the beginning of your new marriage given your drug issues?

John McAfee: Rocky. I was on the edge of the precipice with drugs and alcohol at Omex. You just have no idea how insane Silicon Valley was at that time. People were making money left and right; one month's salary after tax could buy you a house, and a good engineer capable of writing a serviceable operating system could write their own ticket.

The wider economy in America was booming at the time. Meanwhile, the demand for the technology was impossibly high while the supply was impossibly low. Why? Because this was a whole new fucking field, and only we—those of us who had been in programming from the beginning—knew how to play on it. It was quite a time.

At this point, it's important to say that, as many drugs as there were flowing around in 1983, substances like cocaine actually had a purpose. We were all on the edge of an exciting moment for mankind. The dawning of the computer age was imminent. We needed these drugs to keep functioning for as many hours as possible so we could keep making breakthroughs. These advances were going to change the world. And they did. Nothing changed the world like computer technology. Drugs, especially stimulants, were an essential part of that.

ME: You've told me before that you have a good sense of impending doom. Did you have that sense in 1983?

John McAfee: Methamphetamine's appearance in the valley changed a lot of things. Relative to cocaine, methamphetamine is a vastly superior stimulant for everything: staying awake, concentration, and coming down hard. No comedown is harder than methamphetamine. So when you're working with brilliant people, half of whom are constantly wired, edgy, and ragged, it eventually takes its toll. In that environment, I did what I always did and just took things to the absolute limit and beyond. I have no clue how work ever got done in that office. Perhaps as a distraction, I also got into the Bay Area sex club scene around that time.

ME: What was the impetus for going down that path as a newly married man?

John McAfee: Just the people who were around me. Jeff, who I mentioned earlier, was into tantric sex as well as taking all manner of drugs. He and his girlfriend were running around, sleeping with other couples and belonging to sex clubs. Meanwhile, another programmer who worked with me at Omex, Rich, was also into the San Francisco club scene, and I'd known him for several years after our paths crossed at one of my previous employers.

Rich was one of the brightest men I ever met, but he was also one of the strangest. One night he said to me, "Dude, let's go to The Catacombs in San Francisco," and believe me when I tell you that this place, in the 1980s, was the most experimental sex club on the whole fucking planet. He took me to a party in this huge gothic-looking building with arched ceilings. It looked like a massive cave, and in that cave were things I'd never seen before.

ME: Would you say your sexual tastes were experimental at this point?

John McAfee: Yes—and for two interrelated reasons. Firstly, I'd taken a lot of drugs of various kinds by 1983. Inevitably, I'd had a lot of sex while taking drugs at various times. And some of the sex I'd had while under the influence of psychedelics was indescribable. Secondly, and as a result of that, I was a sex addict. I don't say that glibly at all, or to brag; it was just a fact. Therefore, I was always looking for the next sexual thrill, which meant I was liable to be tempted down extreme paths.

ME: How much do drugs enhance sexual experiences for you?

John McAfee: I have always used drugs with women, and it's a very important part of my life because it's a very potent part of my life. Oh, my God, does it enhance the experience. I could recommend a drug for almost every sensation you want to feel while having sex. If you wanted to feel like God himself is kissing you, I could give you a drug that would let you feel that.

ME: What did you see at The Catacombs?

John McAfee: Even by my standards, The Catacombs was an extreme experience, and it was comprised of various demonstrations, one of which was Mistress Cat, a blond dominatrix from across the bay in Oakland, who gave a demonstration with a young slave. This young slave was a guy in his early twenties, naked, tied up by the wrists and suspended from something above, with his feet just a few inches above the ground. Mistress Cat had a whip and flagellated him as a bit of blood started running down. Then she put on a glove, which appeared to have long, sharp tacks sticking out from the palm and each individual finger, whereupon she reached under, grabbed his whole package, and started to squeeze. Blood was appearing between her fingers as he attempted to pull himself up. The pain must have been indescribable. But his face wasn't one of pain. It exhibited nothing but total ecstasy. That was just an example of the kind of thing that was happening there.

Another was this old man in his seventies who got naked, wrapped chains around himself before prostrating himself beneath a raised stage, in effect making himself a human step for women in high heels. He lay there all night long while women walked all over him as they were going up and down from the stage.

Then there were two gay guys, one of whom was tied up with electrodes attached to his nipples. Meanwhile, the other passed the controller around to anyone who was watching. Many people cranked it up to ten on the dial.

There were hundreds of these demonstrations going on simultaneously. This was the kind of shit that Rich got me into, and it absolutely went hand in hand with the Omex lifestyle vibe.

ME: I know you got sober and clean around this time. Was Omex the tipping point?

JOHN MCAFEE: That kind of lifestyle has a heavy price, let's just say that. And that price is not payable in money, albeit that I did eventually quit my well-paid job at Omex around this time. If I hadn't, I would have self-destructed. For me, it all came to a head one day. I felt like I was standing on a deserted street corner at night, with a cold wind blowing through a big hole in the center of my being. That's the only way I can describe how I was feeling.

ME: In retrospect, do you think this feeling was the culmination of an emotional state that long predated Omex?

JOHN MCAFEE: Yeah. When you're in that kind of state, you always know something's not right. But instead of doing something about it, you take more drugs to see if that makes things any better. Or you might think that if you streamline what you're taking, that might change things enough. But none of these things have an effect when you reach that point on the street corner I'm describing.

ME: I feel like the fact that the street is deserted and you're alone is especially symbolic.

JOHN MCAFEE: Oh, absolutely it is. When you reach that place, believe me, my friend, you are on your own. You certainly don't have friends anymore. They have slipped away over time without you even noticing. There *are* no friends in the world of drugs—this I promise you.

ME: Is that a generalization?

JOHN MCAFEE: Yes, it's a generalization in the sense that it applies to all drugs, including religion, which, in my mind, is a drug as bad as any other. It certainly applies to my life. Maybe nobody else has ever felt as empty and alone as I felt. So I did what everybody did back then, at least those who had the money to: I started going to shrinks. I just kept thinking: *Someone has to know what the fuck is wrong with me.*

I hired and fired about five of them pretty quickly. But every single one of them identified the fact that I had a serious fucking drug problem, which I didn't try to hide. They all said: "Stop taking drugs!"

ME: Had you even tried prior to these shrink meetings?

John McAfee: Fuck yes! This is how bad it had gotten with me. I would flush all my drugs down the toilet at night—every fucking thing. Then, at five o'clock in the morning, I'd be awake and desperately looking for crumbs on the table or for any powder that might have fallen against the windowsill. Meanwhile, I'd be calling everybody I knew, and within hours, I'd have replenished everything I'd flushed down the toilet the night before. I repeated this cycle on countless occasions. The only people I had left in my life were Rich and people I'd just call coke whores.

ME: Were these actual whores?

John McAfee: Not necessarily. This is just the general term for women who would fuck you if you had some really fine cocaine. I had plenty of those, but those weren't real friends any more than the other people who hung around me only because I had drugs were. Any sensible person had abandoned me long ago. I was left hanging out with the dregs of society.

ME: Again, there's a big part of you that is drawn to that underbelly of society, true?

John McAfee: Yes. Whenever I could experience the company of people I never knew existed; I did. These people fascinated me. That, in general, still applies today. If you're in town, and you're that kind of person, I don't care if you're eating children; I want to have dinner with you. And if you are eating children, I *definitely* want to have dinner with you.

So, anyway, by the time I got to my fifth or sixth shrink, I was starting to get really pissed off because none of them could fucking fix me.

I was paying them good money, yet I was still taking drugs and feeling empty. As ludicrous as this might sound, I was looking at them thinking, *What is your fucking problem?*

Finally, I met this older, jolly-looking Santa Claus type. I liked him because he smiled and was jovial. I enjoyed visiting him simply because he seemed to enjoy his job and life generally.

On my second visit, he said, "Mr. McAfee, I can't help you. But call this number please, and go to a meeting." He handed me a card for AA and said, "This, is the only help I can possibly give you." He stood up and walked out. Later, I called the number.

ME: How long before you went to an actual meeting?

JOHN MCAFEE: I went to one that same night in Santa Cruz, even though I knew that alcohol per se, wasn't exactly my problem. When I showed up at this meeting, everybody around me was warm and friendly. They looked in my eyes when they addressed me and genuinely listened when I spoke. So, I sat there and the man beside me reached over and shook my hand, "How do you do, sir?" That was too much for me. I got up, pretty much ran to the door, and left thinking: *This shit is not for me....*

I was standing on the sidewalk by my car when this man came out. He put his arm around my shoulder and said, "Why don't you come back in?" And I did. It was a speaker's meeting that night, where someone in the group would stand up and talk at length. This lesbian woman got up, the last person on Earth I would have anything in common with. For that half an hour that she talked, she told my story exactly—because we all have that story.

ME: I understand that that that's an extremely tough moment to confront.

JOHN MCAFEE: From that day in 1983 up until seven years ago, I never touched any drugs or alcohol. Resisting was the hardest thing I've ever done. But, after about four years, I felt little by way of desire to take drugs or drink. I knew I couldn't possibly slip.

For the first year or two, I went to two AA meetings every day. In the evenings, I would go out to hospitals and mental institutions to help inmates who had issues like mine. Again, these were the people I gravitated to, and the reality was that most of them were only there because they'd fried their brains and lives on drugs and alcohol.

ME: Did you connect specifically with any of these people?

John McAfee: The main reason any one of them went to these meetings in these institutions was that there was always free coffee and cigarettes. You didn't get coffee in a mental institution unless you went to AA meetings, and these were just like regular AA meetings, only the people there were a little crazier.

This one guy who was there told a story about how he went off the edge on methamphetamine three years previously. At that point, they put him on anti-psychosis drugs, which, in many cases, are actually worse than the drugs themselves. "I don't have any hope whatsoever for my future," he began, "because I can't, given the drugs they are giving me, ever articulate myself well enough to ever be allowed to leave here." Basically, unless he got out of there, which he couldn't, he'd never get off these anti-psychotic drugs. I really got to see some things that opened my eyes.

I went to this one meeting in that first year in South San Jose, where it was basically the resident Mexican population that showed up. When there were gringos there, they held the meeting in English. When there were no gringos, they held the meetings in Spanish.

I walked in there one night in 1984, and this man stood up and told a story about how he was a blackout drinker who had a tendency to get violent, and that he woke up one morning to find that his wife was gone. There was blood around the house; he didn't know what had happened. Then he found her in the garage in a garbage bag, chopped into pieces, which, as it turned out, he had himself done. He had gone to prison for that and had gotten out after so many years, and there he was with me, telling his story.

ME: How did that story make you feel?

JOHN MCAFEE: If you start hearing stories like that, well, motherfucking hell, you will start paying attention to your own life.

ME: Do you think these AA meetings gave you a sense of camaraderie that you had never really had?

JOHN MCAFEE: Yes. I needed real people I could listen to and who would listen to me. Everyone in the technology business back then was a fake and was puffing up, polishing their image, smiling for the sake of smiling, and talking vacuous shit. They weren't talking about finding their own wife chopped up in garbage bags. That's a real fucking conversation, my friend. I heard some real shit at AA.

ME: Can you explain how AA made life more navigable for you in particular?

JOHN MCAFEE: Early on, I had the revelation that the addiction wasn't to a physical substance but to a state of being. I realized for the first time in my life that we're all basically the same. We are all self-centered. I am a self-centered motherfucker. And so are you. AA didn't change that, but what it did do was promote the acceptance of that.

At the time, when I accepted that fact about myself, that allowed me to accept it in everybody else. And what a major jump that is in a person's relationship with the world. We are all in the same fucking boat. We are lost, many of us. We are alone, many of us.

AA totally changed my life, but at the same time, it confined my life because you cannot live always based on principles. There are no principles in a war, or when someone is trying to kill you or kidnap or abuse you. In those situations, principles go out the window; it becomes life or death. And when the shit really hit the fan, and I went to AA, I realized that I didn't need principles anyway.

Therefore, now, I do exactly what I want, with no exception. Obviously, I don't want to do things that are harmful to myself or others, but that's only because I'm still living. But if the need arises, I'm drinking. If the need arises, I promise you I'm taking methamphetamine. And the need for both has arisen on several occasions in the last eight years. But for the rest of the time, I can take or leave both drugs and alcohol.

ME: I've sensed a theme of loneliness that runs through your life. Would that be a fair comment?

John McAfee: We are all alone. I don't give a shit what anyone else says; we are. If you think, just by virtue of the fact that you're in a crowded auditorium that somehow, you're not alone, well you don't understand what alone really means. You are on your own, people. I don't care who is around you.

However, as long as other people's goals, desires, and hopes are aligned with ours, we experience what we think are camaraderie and friendship. If at any point that alignment ceases, that so-called friendship also ceases. This I know to be a fact.

It's like being on a train where everyone's cool with the destination. Nobody is dragging his or her feet because everyone just wants to get there. But when that train breaks down or gets to the other end, that's when you're going to find out who your fucking friends are. To that extent, your so-called friends are an ever-changing and oscillating set of individuals that is entirely dependent on your trajectory relative to theirs. Does that sound cynical?

ME: No. But when you get there, it makes life easier and not harder, yes?

John McAfee: Absolutely. It makes life perfect. It makes things like forgiveness so much easier. How could you not forgive someone who has done exactly what you would have done yourself? Please, God, let's all get real. That changes everything how about how you view life, and it is also a healthy attitude for business. Having gone through every aspect of drug ingestion and the motives behind taking them, I really understood that aspect of human nature at a time when I most needed to.

ME: Why do you think so many people can't face their own realities and, by extension, can't stop addictive behaviors?

John McAfee: That's a great question, and I really believe that the reason is that we, as humans, spend a lot of time judging other human beings. That's what we do. Judging other people simply allows us to put ourselves in whatever position we want to, in terms of where we fit into the social order: strongest, fastest, slickest, coolest, or whatever. And that becomes a fundamental part of our reality: our perception of our place on the social scale. And we can only ever find that place by judging others.

ME: But none of that is real....

John McAfee: The opposite. That shit is as fake as it gets. But it's real enough in our minds that we structure our reality around it. Now, when people start looking at themselves, the first thing that they realize is that the people we hate the most, we hate because we are exactly the same. And to accept that, we must destroy our entire worldview. If we can't accept that we are the things we hate most, and that we have a roaring fire inside of us no matter how that fucking fire manifests, we can't move forward. So, for me, in 1984, I had to destroy everything about my perception of the reality I lived in.

ME: On paper, that's seems like a monumental achievement.

John McAfee: Don't get me wrong: everybody is capable of this. But not everybody is placed in a situation where this absolutely has to happen. If you're in a fucking jungle and bullets are flying over your head, there's not much force needed to let you see how bad your situation is. In my case, the trajectory of my life just happened to pass through this big ass room full of mirrors. The world had put me in front of a mirror, my mirror—the mirror of John McAfee—in which I had no choice but to see myself. If I hadn't, I'd be dead.

ME: What specifically did you see in that mirror?

John McAfee: All the ugliness that I'd ever hated. It was me, and it was also everybody. Seeing yourself is only half the battle though. Learning how to accept and love the part you hate is the real job. But you have to, because it's the truth of you!

ME: What is the truth of you?

John McAfee: Before AA, I was a divided human being. One half did not communicate with the other. Each knew the other was there but chose to glance over and say, "Nah, fuck you."

Until 1984, I had never acted as a whole person. If you can't accept yourself as a whole person, you sure as hell can't act like one. But now I do. In everything I do, I see my generosity and my greed; I see my love and my dislike. I see everything. As of right now, I am a gracious, compassionate, loving, generous, hopeful human being. I am also a greedy, angry, jealous, selfish human being. I am all of that simultaneously, and there is not a single word, a single act, or a single thought that I could have that does not simultaneously conclude all these things.

Not only do I see everything, but I also realized that everything we call negative has a use. It is either life-supporting, life-preserving, or somehow enhances our ability to perceive, discriminate, or understand. Take anger, for example. People say it's just ugly, but I see anger as a beautiful tool that is entirely necessary. If you were to tell your kid not to touch a hot stove with his or her hand, for example, what are you going to do when he or she reaches for that stove? An angry word or phrase is going to get their fucking attention, that's for sure.

ME: Many would say that religion created this division.

John McAfee: Let's not blame religion entirely, please. But society as a collective, where words like schools, parents, and neighbors, etc., only exist as part of that society, can only function if two things happen. One, you know who you are and that the negative parts of you are not going to hurt other people.

Or you're not that whole person, and society, in the form of your parents, has to force you to conform by saying, "This is bad"; "Don't do that"; "Don't do it this way." And then, when you leave home, you are forced in another way by the cops who say: "Dude, do that, and you are going to jail."

It's one of those two alternatives, and since not everyone is able to be a whole person, that's where the structure of society gives us the concept of shame, which becomes significant when the threat of punishment alone just isn't enough of a deterrent to keep people in line. Punishment *and* shame are what society uses to keep people in check, and it is shame that makes us divide ourselves in two. And…to circle back to your point, it is religion that is the main propagator of shame—"*Shame* on you…."

Society *needs* religion, or something like it, to provide the shame, which, in turn, keeps society orderly. However, I don't feel shame. That should be blatantly obvious to the most casual observer. I have never avoided a question for the last thirty-five years, unless you ask me something like, "Hey, are you into kinky sex?" In which case, I'll say, "None of your fucking business." I wouldn't be saying that from a place of anger either, but more from a societal perspective of telling you to get back in line!

ME: Maybe this idea of acknowledging our two sides is something we are all meant to find out about life?

John McAfee: I do not know what life is all about. But I do know that it's not possible to act as a whole human being, as an *individual,* if you don't love all of yourself, the two distinct sides of you. Beyond that, I don't think love for anyone or anything in this world is possible if you don't love yourself.

For me, everything in my past that I thought was love was simply self-interest. If I loved a woman, what did that mean? Well, it meant I wanted to keep her, for my own pleasure and joy. All the time I was with her, I was on cloud fucking nine. But, fuck me, don't lose that bitch. That's not love. But now I actually can love people. I love the people who steal from me. It's crazy. I also love the people who don't—because they are all just me. As soon as I fell in love with myself, I fell in love with the universe because I realized I knew who I am. The dogs who come up and lick me in the street, or don't; I am them.

ME: What was the next job after Omex and these days in AA?

John McAfee: I'm glad we talked about how I feel about relationships. I don't think I've ever articulated it before. Anyway, yes, so I went from Omex to a job at Lockheed Martin, and at Lockheed, I did exactly the same thing as I ever did, with the notable difference being that I was in the midst of attending daily AA meetings. But again, my reputation was so good, my design ethic so strong, and my code so tight, that I got away with it. Nobody even bothered anymore. I told them I'd be working from home before I even took the job.

While I was at Lockheed, because I was bored working from home, I started a whole bunch of businesses of my own, one of them called Voice Command, which was the first off-the-shelf voice recognition product. I ended up selling it to Interstate Voice Products for $800,000, which was a lot of money in 1984. That was my first truly entrepreneurial product in computers that made me significant money.

ME: What was the progression into forming McAfee from Lockheed?

John McAfee: Well, as I told you, it was during this period at Lockheed where I got pulled to the side to work on the CIA Black program following that thorough interrogation where I told you I answered as honestly as I possibly could. The Black program itself was unremarkable, but just like anyone else who has worked on one, I was told of the dire consequences I'd face if I ever discussed it.

People might say, "Well, you are a fugitive now. Why won't you just say what you did?" My response to that would simply be that I'd like to hope that I won't always be in this position. Like I said, the work was secret but unremarkable, and it took many years until the results of the work I did became useful.

Beyond that, the lines between Lockheed and my starting McAfee were extremely blurred, because, as usual, I was working from home and not from the office, I'd essentially started McAfee, or certainly started developing some of the aspects that would underpin it, while I was still supposed to be working for Lockheed. I was making more money from my side-gigs than I was from my main job, and my Lockheed salary was far from insignificant by any normal standards.

As usual, I just pushed the boundaries of my relationship with my employer as far as they could possibly be pushed. I was never fired from Lockheed. I'd describe my move away as more of a slow degradation. I did progressively less and less to the point where I did nothing at all. It became this absurd position whereby I was so busy with my own business that I never had time to show up at meetings for my day job and just quit.

SEVEN

JERUSALEM

In almost all the interviews and articles I'd read, McAfee had been quick to take credit for the development of what was the world's first antivirus software. Given what he'd told me about his prowess at the various companies he'd worked for up until the early 1980s, it was obvious that the man had a seriously able programming brain that was capable of solving pretty much any problem in that realm, and with the minimum of effort.

However, I had also read that there were other important figures in the early days of McAfee. One of them had been mentioned in a newspaper article and in a web article written by McAfee himself. In both, he stopped just short of saying that it was this man who'd actually unlocked the secrets of some of the first computer viruses. As we delved into the McAfee Associates era, I did so curious as to whether he'd discuss this man's involvement at all, far less credit him, for truly vital work done at the dawn of the computer age.

ME: Do you remember the first time you ever heard about a computer virus?

JOHN MCAFEE: Vividly. I was sitting at my kitchen table in Santa Clara sometime in 1986 when my brother-in-law Neil called. "You need to read the paper today," he said. "There's a story that might interest you."

He was referring to a little article tucked away in a corner of the *San Jose Mercury* that was talking about a virus that could affect computers. It was called the Brain virus, and it had seemingly originated in Pakistan courtesy of two hacker brothers in Lahore who owned a small computer repair shop.

My first reaction was probably much like anyone else's around that time—*What the fuck?* Nobody had even heard the term "computer virus" before.

As I read on, the article explained how the virus replicated itself like a real, living entity, moving from disc to disc, machine to machine, infecting systems as it went. From a technological perspective, I was impressed and fascinated at the same time. And, more than anything, I really wanted to know how they'd done it. Then my own intuitive programming brain took over. Before too long, it became clear to me how they'd done it.

I thought, *I can solve that shit.*

ME: This was clearly virgin territory. How do you even start trying to address a completely new problem like this?

JOHN MCAFEE: I decided to design a little program that could remove it and, in effect, kill it and repair the damage, with the help of a programming friend of mine named Dennis Yelle.

My first contact with Dennis had been back when I was running Homebase, an early incarnation of my bulletin board. Although it had something of an audience in Silicon Valley, this bulletin board was really just a hobby, simply something to entertain myself with because there was nothing else to do at night, given that there were no movies on TV, etc.

I began to notice that Dennis was a very active member of the community that frequented this board, but never in a social sense. Where others might shoot the shit from time to time by discussing subjects outside of computer technology, he'd only ever go on there and say something along the lines of: "Has anyone seen the second version of PK unzip? I heard it was out, but it's not up here."

I would then respond: "Oh, fuck. Sorry, I meant to release that new file set earlier," and I'd put it up there. He was a complete anomaly.

ME: It sounds to me as if you were willing to look beyond this guy's personality to get to his programming ability?

John McAfee: Yes, and one day, I got a private message.

"Your clock is off."

It was Dennis.

"What clock?"

"Your computer clock."

On checking, my computer clock was indeed something like two hundred goddamn milliseconds fast.

"You've got a broken clock. Fix it."

"But Dennis, I don't know how. I'm a software person. I have no idea how to fix the system clock."

He clearly mulled this over for a while. Then, an hour later, another message came in.

"I'll fix it."

"OK. When do you want to come?"

"Now."

Evidently, this was a burning fucking issue for this man. He simply could not log on to my bulletin board and see my system time different from his.

I gave him my address.

ME: What did you expect? When did you hear from him next?

John McAfee: Twenty minutes later, this old beat-up Ford pulled up outside my fucking house! A man got out, skinny, hair that was long and, as he approached, I realized had more than likely never been washed. He had a face that you'd expect to accompany long and stringy hair that had never been washed: a mixture of historic pockmarks and current pustules, framed by thick glasses.

After he stepped out of his car, this man stared only at the ground as he walked towards the house and knocked on the door. I opened it. He did not introduce himself and did not at any point look me in the eye.

"Where's the computer?" he said.

I pointed him in the direction, and he walked over with his shoulder bag, unzipped it, and started getting out screwdrivers. He popped the case off, removed the chip with a pair of pliers, and replaced it with another from a zippy bag. He then reassembled everything, turned the machine on, and stared at it.

"OK."

He closed his bag, walked past me without saying goodbye, without saying *anything.* I opened the door for him, he walked out, got in his car, and drove off. That was my first meeting with Dennis Yelle.

ME: He was clearly an eccentric introvert. Did you consider hiring him formally?

John McAfee: Absolutely. Right then, I realized why this man was so smart in the electronic world. He had nothing else. There *were* no other smarts in this man. He had no other means to interact with the world other than via his computer.

It was a no-brainer to hire him. And as time passed, it became obvious to me that Dennis possessed a level of programming ability that I'd never seen before and have never come across since. I'd been managing software engineers for many years, yet I'd never seen anyone whose code was, on one hand, so neat but also so completely free from bugs. Never, in all the time I knew him, did his work contain a single bug.

Dennis Yelle was the programming equivalent of people you hear about who have the ability to multiply one-hundred-digit numbers in their heads. His work was always *perfection*. Good God, what's that worth? He was worth a hundred of the best programmers who have ever worked for me.

Not only was it imperative that I hired Dennis, but it also became clear to me that I needed to give him whatever he fucking wanted, whenever he wanted it. If he called and told me that his disc was fried and that he needed a new one, I'd drop everything and get him a new disc, all the time putting up with his vagaries like him calling me but then refusing to answer the door when I went round to his apartment.

Several times, I called round with something and ended up leaving it on the doormat because he wouldn't come to the door. He knew I'd put it there, of course, because I'd seen him watch me through thinly parted window curtains. *OK, I get it,* I eventually thought to myself. These weird idiosyncrasies became unimportant to me. What was important was that Dennis got what he needed to do the work.

ME: How long did it take to get to grips with the Brain virus?

John McAfee: On reflection, the Brain virus was a simple enough concept. It soon became apparent that the virus only affected the boot sector of discs, meaning, as soon as you turned a computer on, the virus went into the memory and initialized the operating system. It was then, in effect, in control of that operating system. That was the extent of its modus operandi, however. Its controlling influence was limited to the hard disc.

The hackers had achieved this by, in essence, copying the original boot sector and putting it in a safe place where it could do no damage but could still be accessed. They then replaced that boot sector with the virus, whereupon they could take charge and make a bunch of modifications and rearrangements. Then they loaded and restored the original boot sector.

It was smart, but there was a flaw. The original boot sector was in a place we could access because we could find its location within the code, the programming language needed to create the Brain virus. Once we knew that, all we needed to do was find it and restore it to its original state.

So, with Dennis's input, I quickly designed what would be the first virus-scan program to counter the Brain virus, and I put it up on my bulletin board.

ME: Would you define that as being the moment virus scanning became a business of sorts? Was this ground zero for McAfee?

John McAfee: By this time, I had the largest, most active programming bulletin board in Silicon Valley, and I was managing it all from just a tiny corner of my living room. Anyone who had a phone number could use this bulletin board by dialing in to a rollover number. I had the ability to juggle thirty-two simultaneous board "visitors" courtesy of the same number of phone lines that were snaking their way into my house. It was all a bit clunky, but it was the only means we had of exchanging information in 1986. A freely available and useable internet was still several years away.

Regardless, within just a few days, my virus scanner was on a million or more computers. I was the first to utilize the concept of shareware. Now everybody does it. All a user had to do was run it, and the program would then tell them whether or not his or her computer was infected. If it was, they were given the option to fix it. If it wasn't, no foul.

It was that simple, and it was an instant solution, free of charge. However, just a month later, I caught a glimpse of a frightening future when another virus appeared.

ME: Was this expected? Did you foresee a lengthy battle between you and the hackers?

John McAfee: It certainly seemed like there was intent to pose increasingly complex problems. A virus-like Brain that infected the boot sector was one idea, and one that while clever was also limited in scope. A far more deadly idea was a virus that infected the computer's programs themselves. To that extent, this new virus called Jerusalem was a completely different class of infection, with a totally different way of propagating. Where Brain's code was visible and accessible, Jerusalem infected programs in a manner whereby the actual code itself was being changed.

The hackers had somehow managed to alter the code of a program while still allowing it to ostensibly run and function, albeit under the control of the virus's DNA rather than its own. That was a whole new world of problems, given that every computer program is a unique entity with its own specific DNA signature. As if that wasn't bad enough, there was the worrying possibility a virus of this kind could be hidden inside the programs in a manner that maybe we couldn't detect.

With Jerusalem, we had to dig deep into its DNA because of its potential to affect hundreds and thousands of programs at a time. It became a job of great magnitude, and there was only me and three other programmers with the relevant knowledge. And even once we figured it out, we still had to go about establishing firstly what damage the virus had done and, secondly, whether we could repair it.

This was when things really started getting fun. I knew right there and then that unless somebody came up with a solution that could counter this onslaught of new viruses, the future for computers looked disastrous. An arms race of sorts ensued.

On one side of the fence, once the concept hit the minds of the hacking community, there soon loomed a dark legion of would-be hackers that probably numbered many tens of thousands. Many of them were just bored kids who enjoyed hacking in the same way as their friends liked to spray paint the sides of buildings with their own unique tags. The difference was that, instead of affecting people in their own town with a spray can, computer hackers could fuck with people all over the world.

Meanwhile, on our side, we were just manically trying to repel wave after wave of attacks. It genuinely felt like we were in a war, and there was a tangible urgency that we all knew we could not step down from. It wasn't a job. Without sounding too dramatic, it was a fight for the future of mankind at the dawn of the electronic age.

All of this work was being done in fractions of seconds, and it was, without question, the most exciting, adventurous period of my life. During this time, I rarely slept, worked seventeen or eighteen hours every day, seven days a week. I ate while working and sometimes slept while working, simply because I couldn't keep my eyes open.

ME: What did your wife make of all of this?

John McAfee: She wasn't happy. Linda eventually took charge. "I'm not living like this," she said. "You need to get an office."

As they say, something had to give. She was either going to leave, or she was going to make us leave! Granted, everything had gotten a tad hectic in our house. Everybody that worked for me was basically living with us. We'd had no time to even consider more formal business arrangements, to the extent that one of the women who worked for me was using the top of a washing machine for a makeshift desk.

But the truth is that trivialities of that kind just didn't matter to any of us in these early months. We were all in it together, fighting the good fight to hold up the virus world on our own. Meanwhile, Norton and everyone else were still just barely gearing up to get their own products out. It took some of them years, and, in many cases, they had to pack their product in a box and sell it in a store. At the beginning, we were *it*—lone soldiers in the field.

Linda soon acquired us some office space that could accommodate twenty or so people, very close to the house. It had to be within walking distance; we were all so busy that none of us could afford to spend ten or twenty minutes of our day commuting anywhere. She literally moved our asses out of the house, mattresses from the floor and all, in one day. Now we were ready.

ME: This would have been 1987 and the beginning of McAfee Associates as a formal company, yes?

JOHN MCAFEE: Yes, and the business really took off. Within the first year and a half, although the products were free to use for regular individuals, we were accumulating vast sums of money by charging corporations a sizeable license fee. We were their only salvation at the time, and they were prepared to pay handsomely for it. It felt like there was this huge hole in the office ceiling into which money was raining into a bucket.

Yet, because we were barely paying ourselves a salary, we had nothing to spend this money on other than food. We dare not hire another developer because that would mean that one of us would have to be missing in action while the new recruit was trained.

So we continued, while Linda, now bored because she rarely saw me, ironically, started spending some of the company's proceeds on a new car and a four million dollar cliff-top mansion in Santa Cruz that was acquired in an auction after one of the financiers who got caught up in the savings and loans scandal had it seized. I barely set foot in the house before we bought it. I just didn't have the time. Only occasionally did my mind wander away from the work long enough for me to think: *Jesus, we're making serious money.*

As an aside, the reason we didn't charge individual users anything was that we didn't offer technical support. And the reason we didn't offer technical support was that we didn't have the capacity to answer the telephone. We had millions of individual users by that point. It wouldn't have been possible. So, basically, my corporate message was this: *I'll give you our product and all future updates for free. In return, you promise never to fucking call me.*

ME: I have to say this is a strange approach to customer service for a new company in the service industry, no?

John McAfee: We had no fucking choice! I wasn't answering the telephone every five fucking minutes. But there were some phone calls we just had to answer. Firstly, we had to have some capacity to take new orders from large corporations. Thereafter, it was quick and low maintenance to take on a new client. All we'd then do was send them a contract to sign and thereafter we sent them a disc that they were free to copy however many times they wanted in return for, in some cases, $100,000 for what was called a site license, based on the total number of machines within that organization.

Secondly, we wanted to get into a position whereby every large corporation had a designated phone contact in our office in the event of a virus incident. Why? Because we needed every scrap of information they might have about any new viruses that were doing the rounds. These were telephone calls we definitely did pick up, and I tasked Linda with hiring a bunch of people who could fulfill these two vital support functions that would allow us to stay ahead.

Consequently, information about new viruses poured in during these early years of the company. In every case, it was imperative that we accessed these new viruses as quickly as possible and took them apart to study the DNA makeup of each, all the time checking for code that might resemble a prior virus given that it was becoming common for hackers to take an old virus and add something to it.

In most cases, these recyclers would leave something of the original code. These fragments were what we'd see when we did a scan. All these snippets themselves might have appeared harmless, but the fact that they were there at all meant that we were missing something and had to dig deeper until we located the DNA of the real virus. Then it was game over. We'd have a fix within two hours, and our updates then moved like wildfire. Again, our distribution methodology was truly unsurpassed.

ME: This was the birth of the hacking community?

John McAfee: On reflection, it was around this time that personalities started to appear in the hacking world, for sure. It got to a point where we'd created an imaginary Top 25, not that we knew any of their names. Instead, we could recognize their style, the smoothness or the shagginess of the code, and the general sophistication of the programming talent on display. Every hacker had his or her subtle nuances that soon became office lore.

"This one's an Igor...."

"Here's another Korivinsky!"

"Guys, I've found an Ivan variant over here."

All we knew were that most of these early viruses were of Russian origin as, let's face it, at that time, Russia had most of the best programmers.

ME: Was it only Russians at this point?

John McAfee: At the beginning, that's all we knew about. However, sometime in 1990, a hacker in Germany created the first encrypted virus called The Whale. Again, this was a completely new concept because, suddenly, a way had been found to make every copy of the virus completely different. Consequently, on every program that was infected, there was nothing that resembled the virus's original DNA after encryption was run.

When this virus first showed up, the whole office was freaking the fuck out. For the first day, all we did was sit there and watch it replicate, like some kind of alien spawn. But there was a method to this temporary paralysis. We did so because we had to observe both its means of replication and how randomly it did so.

In tandem, we also wanted to monitor the damage caused as well as any signs of the virus trying to leave a computer to enter another, whether that was via a floppy disk or some kind of electronic communication with the bulletin board. While there was little by way of connectivity back then by today's fluid standards, there was just enough for a virus to sneak out of a machine somehow.

While we were watching these moves and manipulations, Dennis Yelle was already taking The Whale apart in his own, unique sociopathic way. We never knew exactly where he was, but he always reappeared when he had something. In all his time at the company, he only ever addressed me.

"You'll never, ever find the DNA of this virus if that's what you're looking for first," he explained, never making eye contact. I don't think I ever saw his eyes. Dennis then went on to explain that the hackers had to have written a decryption module. Without the ability to be unencrypted, he said, the virus could not have worked. It, therefore, had to always carry with it its decryptor, which in turn couldn't be encrypted.

"Here is the DNA of the decryption module…." Dennis then said.

Eureka!

ME: How long did that process take?

John McAfee: All of this happened in about a day and a half, not fast enough that we didn't all lose sleep, but quick enough that we still had an update ready to go in three days from first discovery. But that wasn't the end of the matter.

Six months after that first encrypted virus, another appeared that had a totally new concept of encryption in which, every time the program infected another, the infected program was subject to a different decryption technique with a completely different DNA. This way, no two would ever be the same.

When I saw it, I thought, *This has to be the same creator as The Whale.*

As a group, we thought the hackers had invented the equivalent of the nuclear bomb. We genuinely thought it was the end. There appeared to be far too many complexities, and there was no doubt that the answers, if they existed at all, lay many layers deep into the darkness of programming. This was a place where the challenges were no longer recognizable to the average eight-hour-per-day programmer. We were dealing with shit so subtle and yet still so harmful, that we had never even dreamed of it. We learned more from the virus writers in those first few years than I had in the totality of my career. There was definitely a degree of respect for the people creating these viruses.

ME: How much advantage did being clean and sober give you?

John McAfee: I couldn't have done it if I wasn't clean and sober. Not only that, it gave me a real advantage when it came to doing deals with people in the Valley. Having spent years drinking and taking drugs myself, I knew what people's habits were. When I was selling my own white-label products in parallel with running McAfee, I was meeting people all the time, and if it was truly an important meeting, I'd make sure to insist that the only time I was available was 7 p.m. on a Friday evening. I suggested this time because I knew that everybody would be downtown drinking something at the very least, and probably running to the bathroom to snort cocaine. Meanwhile, I was totally fucking sober and totally clean.

When these people started talking business up front, I'd always say, "Please, it has been a long week. Can we just enjoy our dinner and talk business after?" I said this because I knew they weren't drunk enough up front. But by the time we'd had dinner and they'd had nine drinks and been to the bathroom three times to snort coke, I was ready to talk business. Suddenly, I owned the fucking table. I could manipulate people and their decisions.

I did business with this one person from a company in Los Angeles. It was a really important deal for the company; the company's name doesn't matter. Anyway, this guy signed the fucking contract at the dinner table, and when he got back to LA, his boss looked at the contract and said, "What on the fucking Earth have you done? By signing this, you have given the keys to the company to this man."

I'm not certain if the guy got fired or not, but there were definitely advantages to being clean and sober. If you are clean and sober in this world and have half a brain, you will clean up. That's just a fact of life.

ME: Were there any disadvantages?

John McAfee: It was a bit boring being in places where people were drinking, and I wasn't. And yet, it was required in order to both do business and to socialize with any friends that I had, all of whom were totally shocked that I had managed to quit these vices, albeit some of them would eventually get clean themselves later down the line.

ME: As this business developed, was it what you wanted?

John McAfee: McAfee was thrust upon me. I didn't seek it out. A set of circumstances arose in this chaotic world where I was forced to act. At no time was I especially in love with the business or motivated by the money aspect. No, I was simply in love with the act of stopping these motherfuckers. Don't get me wrong: I didn't dislike these hackers. I understood why they were doing what they did, and in different circumstances, I might well have been one of them. Nevertheless, it was a chess game on a monumental scale, and I'd always loved games, almost as much as I loved sex.

ME: Where did the Michelangelo virus fit into this chess game?

John McAfee: Michelangelo was probably the last great problem we had to solve around the time when everything peaked in around 1992. Its potential infection rate was the highest of any virus that we'd ever seen. Machines around the world were acting very strangely in 1992, reports from users were pouring in. We had a copy and were the first to identify what was happening as the work of a virus. We just couldn't let it reach its activation date. It would have shut the computer world down simultaneously. That would have been unheard of.

Normally, viruses would infect a program or a boot sector, and in order to do that, they would make themselves memory resonant and then just wait for an application to run. It didn't matter what that application was, because once the virus was in the memory, it could wait and take control by stopping the problem from working. Michelangelo was the first virus that didn't even wait around until a user randomly used an application, like a word processor, before saying, *Aha, that's the one I was waiting for.* No, it got into the memory, then into your file system, and from there, it started looking for all executable modules. It infected them all at once—every fucking one.

ME: How much of a threat was this particular virus for you guys?

John McAfee: Good God almighty, we'd never seen such a thing. Previously, it took viruses weeks to find the right program to infect or even to move itself. Consequently, few viruses had managed to infect more than 200,000 computers before we stopped them by shipping out software that could be installed to snuff them out. But this thing had the potential to move itself across the world in a matter of days. It could have been nonstop. We had no idea how many users Michelangelo could get to, so we put out an urgent alert.

ME: What was the thinking behind that?

John McAfee: Basically, we did a colossal PR blitz with our software to our customers and the press. We literally gave away millions of discs, including to people who weren't even license holders. Everyone got the disc for free. As a result, we stopped it, to the extent that on the day that it was supposed to activate, there were fewer than two hundred reports of it activating in the world.

ME: Didn't the press give you a hard time about all this?

John McAfee: Yes, they accused me of making a big deal out of it for the benefit of the company. They were implying that there had never really been a threat in the first place. "You spoke of a catastrophic event that just never happened," they said. "Thank God," I said. That's why I went to both the press and my customers at the outset and said, "There will come a day when a virus shuts everything down. I have a free solution right here. Please, God, everybody must run this disk." And pretty much everyone did. Running our program had killed the virus before it even activated. If anything, I was surprised there had even been two hundred incidences. Not only that, our software made sure that the virus couldn't come back in later.

ME: Did there come a time when the frenetic nature of the initial years calmed down from a virus writing perspective?

John McAfee: I recall that this was contentious at the time, but I hired two ex-virus writers—I might not name either of them—to work for us. They'd been having fun fighting us, but they hadn't made a fucking dime while they were doing it. There was serious money on our side, and so, virus writers gradually started defecting. The way I saw it, if they had the talent to write a virus, I wanted them working for us. That solved the problem of having to train someone in a programming science that was brand new and so inherently complex. It would have been easier to train someone in how to get to the fucking moon.

ME: Why won't you name them?

JOHN MCAFEE: One of these ex-virus writers was an eccentric dude also. His name was Ray from New York. He'd written viruses and various other pieces of shit, all of which we'd shut down. Eventually, he said, "Will you hire me?" "Why not?" I said, and the next thing I know, he showed up at the office on a fucking bicycle, which obviously he had not ridden from New York.

Ray was another oddball, but not quite in the same league as Dennis Yelle. He was sociable, heavyset, wore thick glasses, but point blank refused to work in daylight. He only ever came into the office at night, whereupon he drank nothing but Diet Pepsi, to the point that I came in one night to find that the door to his office had been removed and replaced with a new door made of Diet Pepsi cans that had been glued together.

When I actually entered his office, it was in total darkness except for his computer screen, which had the brightness turned up to the maximum. Meanwhile, he was wearing dark glasses. "May I ask why you do this, Ray?" I asked. "Let me show you," he said. I went around, he put his glasses on me, and I couldn't even see the computer or the screen. All I saw, and these were the days before graphic images, were words, which looked as if they were suspended in fucking space. "Cool, right?" he said. Ray was a good, jolly-natured guy but very eccentric.

Anyway, when these defections happened, the war started very heavily tilting in our favor. The dark side reached a pinnacle in about 1992/1993, and thereafter, there was little in the way of people developing threatening computer viruses that extended much beyond occasional isolated breakouts. Meanwhile, there was everything new available in the world of electronic communication security. That's where I was at dead center. I was the man.

However, once the best developers were working for me, I started going home over the hill to our house for a night here and there, even a weekend, confident in the certainty that those people who were still working in the office had things under control. If anything went south when I wasn't there, they just called Dennis Yelle, who insisted on working from home, which was both fine by me, and fine for everyone else because Dennis was such a strange man anyway.

ME: So, on reflection, do you think you envisaged leaving long before you did?

John McAfee: If I'm honest, I started losing interest when that battle started to relent. It was as if I enjoyed the initial stages, the heat of conflict, but once it was over, I had little interest in the thought of the corporate world that I knew would follow thereafter. As I've said many times, that was the last kind of life I ever wanted.

So, I guess in around 1992, I started seeing other things that weren't related to work, like my sexy wife and our beautiful home. I started noticing the fruits of the money I'd almost not noticed making. By 1992 or so, I think we had around fifty million in cash in the bank, and it was then that I realized I could do whatever I wanted and go wherever I felt like going. I started thinking, *I don't even need to be in the office 24/7 anymore.*

ME: How did McAfee get from being a company selling technology to other companies to selling products straight to consumers?

John McAfee: That came after I left, really. Good God, would you want to be in the business of selling a thirty-nine-dollar product to fifty million people? Or would you rather sell a fifty-million-dollar product to thirty-nine people? The marketing people kept saying to me, "Come on, we can sell more product." Meanwhile, all I thought was, *We are going to have to double our staff.* I didn't want all of that; obviously, they did it after I was gone.

Had I stayed, the company would have ruled the world by now because I would have found a way to apply myself out of love for technology. But I fell out of love with the business because it changed into something more corporate and bland. And when I fall out of love with anything, I leave. McAfee was the same. I have loved all the women I've left, right up to the moment I did. I just liked fucking other women too much. With McAfee, I preferred the idea of doing something else too much. That was it.

ME: What kind of other things did you want to do?

JOHN MCAFEE: We'd started chartering yachts to go on boat trips. Linda got me hooked on that whole thing after persuading me to go on a trip with our next-door neighbors in Santa Cruz, who were also extraordinarily wealthy. Initially, I didn't want to do this at all. To charter the yacht for two weeks was going to cost us $400,000 between us, and I just thought, *Why would I want to spend $200,000 to be with these motherfuckers for two weeks?* But, of course, I knew that marriage, as fragile as ours was, was about compromise, so I agreed. Well, I had more fun than anyone on this boat trip. It was one of the best things I'd ever done. From that point on, we did it twice a year for a few years except on future trips, *we* chose the boat, and *we* decided where we went. I always chose the best boats. Some of these things cost $1 million per week.

ME: What did you like about this? And where did you go?

John McAfee: Always the Caribbean somewhere, and I guess I just liked the simplicity of it all. I didn't own the boat, so I didn't need to worry about maintenance, etc. It had a captain and came fully staffed with the finest chefs and sous-chefs ready to serve the best food and the finest wines on the planet. All I had to do was show up. On one trip, I bought two of the most powerful jet skis you could buy and put them on the boat to use on the trip. I used them all the time. There was an enormous sense of freedom derived from blasting off on a powerful jet ski, not from the shore, but from the middle of the ocean.

Jet skiing, therefore, became an important part of my life for a few years from 1993 onwards. My neighbor, Jack, became my regular jet skiing buddy. As well as being sharp as a tack, Jack also had balls of steel. So together, we started this project together.

We wanted to establish cross-ocean jet skiing as a legitimate sport, where people could potentially travel for hundreds of miles across open expanses of ocean. We started out small, hopping over to islands that looked like they might have been five miles away from our boat on these trips we went on. We'd zip there and zip back. We'd be on these machines for hours each day.

Soon, we started getting pretty confident on these things, and then, I came up with an idea: "We jump from island to island coming down here with the boat. Why do we need the boat when we have jet skis?" This was a whole new scale of undertaking. We had to figure out where the nearest piece of land was so that we could work out where we were going. We did that for a couple of trips, and then I said, "We don't need land, Jack."

ME: I guess what you did need was fuel?

John McAfee: To start, we had the biggest Yamaha machines, and these would go 175 miles on a full tank if we were going full fucking bore. But we weren't going full bore. So we were able to drag that range out to 225 miles. Nevertheless, we always built plenty of slack into our planning. We didn't want to be stranded in the middle of the ocean. To me, that would have been my worst nightmare. And when we wanted to go further than one tank would allow, we arranged for the yacht's tender to follow us with spare fuel.

This led to one of the funniest experiences of my life, and by this time, Jack and I were getting seriously cocky. We were both stupid enough and wealthy enough to structure something with yachts, tenders, and jet skis that most people just couldn't do. We wanted to take advantage of that position. We wanted to take this to the max—and our max trip in the Bahamas turned out to be from Exuma to Long Island to Cat Island. We were going for a weather challenge, in big waves and without the tender as backup. Admittedly, we were in an area where, if the jet skis had died for any reason, the currents would have drifted us to Nassau in a day or two. It was dangerous, but there was a safety net of sorts.

Sure enough, we got pounded and pounded by waves for maybe one hundred miles, and then when we turned into the bay at Cat Island, the waves stopped. When we got to the Quay, we were fucking high-fiving and yelling. "This has to be a record, Jack," I said. "The next time we do this we're bringing the press with us."

We walked to the harbormaster's shack, which was the size of a little outhouse. "So where did you boys come from?" he said. "All the way from Exuma," we told him, fucking beaming with pride. He went back into his shack, and I heard him rummaging around, and then he reemerged holding a polaroid photo of a guy with a long beard, on a Yamaha jet ski that was loaded to the fucking brim with fuel bladders, on the front, on the back, and on a little inflatable thing trailing behind. "Yeah," he said, "This guy came in last month." "Oh yeah? Where did he come from?" we asked. "He left Venezuela a month and a half ago!" We couldn't even look at each other after that!

ME: So why did you leave McAfee in the end? When did you cash out?

JOHN MCAFEE: I never cashed out. I just walked away. There's a difference.

ME: Yes, but surely you made money?

JOHN MCAFEE: I made money lots of ways, not least when the company went public in 1992. I got money upfront for that, and there was lots of it. After we went public, I owned the majority share of the stock, but even then, in retrospect, I was slowly and subconsciously uncoupling.

ME: The company went public in 1992, two years before you officially left, is that right?

JOHN MCAFEE: Yes, and there was a story to that. Before we went public, we had to adhere to the most stringent rules of the Securities and Exchange Commission, in addition to those of every other regulatory body. Among these rules was that we all had to prove we were reliable by signing confidentiality agreements that confirmed that we would not talk to anybody about what was happening with the company. They came around with these forms, and Dennis Yelle said, "I'm not signing." He just wouldn't do it.

I went and talked to our venture capital backers. "Dennis Yelle won't sign." "He *has* to," they said. "We can't do this unless he signs."

I was in a position whereby I either had to make Dennis sign a sheet of paper or fire him. But I also knew that if I fired him, we might as well have just shut down the company. We, the venture capitalist backers and me, I mean, had a serious standoff about it. "You all know that he isn't going to talk to anyone," I began. "That motherfucker hardly talks to me! Let's get real for a second, people." "Let's hire him a lawyer," one of the two venture capital backers said.

They got him a lawyer, but then Dennis didn't like the lawyer. So eventually they said to him, "OK, you find a fucking lawyer and we'll pay." He found a lawyer, who turned out to be the most expensive lawyer in all of Silicon Valley. The long and short of it is that it cost $20,000 to get Dennis to sign one piece of paper.

ME: What had been his issue?

John McAfee: Don't know. He just didn't want to sign it. And it didn't even matter what the piece of paper said. But this lawyer was able to talk to him to the point where it was agreed that he was, in fact, his lawyer. But that was all. Thereafter, Dennis refused to talk to him. It was just a fucking nightmare, and an expensive one.

ME: But eventually you orchestrated an exit a year or so later?

John McAfee: Again, the moment I no longer had to watch the horizon like a hawk for danger, I no longer felt necessary. I remember going on one of these boat cruises I mentioned in early 1993 and feeling very stressed all the time, especially with the irritation associated with trying to get in touch with the office on a satellite phone every other day just to say, "Everything OK?" And everything was always fine. We'd talk for a while, and they'd tell me about the virus they'd found the previous night, etc. But basically, the business was running just fine in my absence.

With no requirement to hang on the front lines came freedom. And with freedom came a whole new world. And with that new world came new understandings. I just woke up one day and said to myself, *I don't want this anymore.* I just walked away, giving two weeks of notice. Two months prior, I'd already hired the senior vice president of IBM, a brilliant guy named Bill Larson, to come in as the new CEO. He was a brilliant executive, and it became clear that he had a handle on things and that everything was going to be fine.

ME: What an incredible feeling that must have been?

JOHN MCAFEE: I just didn't want a corporate life of board meetings, legal issues, and talking to corporate people about corporate bullshit. I never wanted that life. Don't get me wrong: I could do that shit; I could do it better than anybody. But I didn't want to spend the rest of my life in an environment where I only existed with people in similar roles, none of whom actually had anything in common with me. That's the thing with the mega-rich. As much as the money seems attractive, the lifestyle that goes with it is not as attractive. The mega-rich really only fraternize with the mega-rich. That was never what I wanted. If anything, I was more comfortable with the underbelly of society and the disenfranchised. To stay at McAfee Associates would have meant denying that part of myself.

ME: Did you keep in touch with anyone after you left?

JOHN MCAFEE: Only ever with the developers. They'd bitch about a new VP of development, or how stupid the modern-day programmers were and how they didn't need to know shit about actual computers like we once did. But I never had any further contact with any of the executive officers. I didn't like any of them.

ME: What happened to Dennis Yelle?

JOHN MCAFEE: He committed suicide maybe ten years after I left. He had nobody that understood him and could not communicate. I did not understand him, but I accepted him 100 percent, which he may have mistaken for understanding. But I was the only person that he ever talked to. I was the only person he ever saw. His was a sad story.

I'll give you an example that'll explain Dennis's lack of understanding. After we'd been working together for a couple of years, I used to get call-outs in Silicon Valley every once in a while to go out and deal with what I could tell from the description on the phone was a brand-new virus. I'd grab Dennis, and we'd hightail it up the highway to San Francisco in a custom Winnebago I'd fitted out with antivirus gear. It was, in effect, an antivirus paramedic unit, and we'd arrive, go in with our mobile gear, get a sample of the virus, and, ideally, fix it on the spot.

We were up there one time, and everyone was panicking and didn't know what to do. I was in the company manager's office, and he was stressing out worrying that he was going to lose his job. I saw a picture on his desk and immediately said, "Are those your kids?" I figured they had to be his kids. "Yeah," he said. "So how old are they?" I continued.

Within twenty seconds, this guy had gone from a state of full panic to absolute calm. On the way back in the car, Dennis turned to me and said, "How did you know how to do that?" "Do what, dude," I asked. "Bringing up the guy's kids. How did you know that would get his interest?" Dennis asked. "Well, they're his kids!" I said.

Dennis simply just did not understand why bringing up this guy's kids would interest him. He was deadly curious about how someone could have that magical ability to bring up a subject of interest. That's how deeply sociopathic that motherfucker was. He was unaware of such simple things. That was Dennis Yelle, an absolutely unique but equally brilliant man.

EIGHT

IN FLIGHT

I have to admit that I was surprised that McAfee had opened up so much about the thing—McAfee Antivirus—that he was arguably most famous for and to which his name will forever be attached. I had always been under the impression that he viewed this part of his life as the least interesting. But what I realized was that it arguably was the part that *was* least interesting. He was, however, perfectly happy to lay it all out for me in terms of how it informed everything he did thereafter.

For him, McAfee wasn't so much of a culmination of a career as it was the beginning of a totally new life. While nobody would ever say that the first forty years of John McAfee's life were pedestrian by any normal standards, relative to what would follow they certainly were.

Regardless, I sensed that he felt relief that he'd talked about the McAfee years and was now out the other side of those conversations. Work, to him, was always something that got in the way of life. And from 1994 onwards, with an estimated $100 million in the bank, John McAfee had every intention of living life to the max, come what may.

••••••••••●••••••••••

John McAfee: Because I'd had no time to do anything apart from work, it was Linda who started our buying spree, while I was still busy working in the final years of McAfee. There we were in this big mansion, on three levels, on a cliff overlooking the ocean in Santa Cruz. We had paid $4 million for it, and it was the most expensive house in Santa Cruz County at that time. There were seven bedrooms and a staff house with three more bedrooms. We weren't going to be able to look after this place, so we started getting people: cleaners, etc., in addition to security, because now people knew who I was and might want to steal from me. Then the next thing Linda said was, "We can't live here and be driving those cars." The next thing I knew, our garage was full of expensive cars, all of them Mercedes. We had almost every model, including one of the only twelve SL 600s in the country at that time. We had all of that shit, and much of this had happened without any input from me. I had been too busy working, while Linda was obviously bored and wanted to do and buy stuff.

ME: Are you saying that your goals and wishes were becoming less aligned?

JOHN MCAFEE: Yes, I think we wanted different things. She wanted to live the life of the super-rich, whereas I was doing everything I could to push away all the things that people think are necessary to support a super-rich lifestyle. I went to no parties, even though I was inevitably invited everywhere. I just had no time for that lifestyle; that lifestyle was all she wanted. We were misaligned. Things were going bad.

I remember one year shortly before I quit working—I can't remember which—when I decided to buy her a brand-new Porsche Boxster convertible as a surprise birthday present. I test-drove all of them, and that motherfucker was the most fun. It was the best car I'd ever driven, albeit that it was the cheapest model in the Porsche range at the time.

On her birthday, this car was delivered to the driveway from a flatbed transporter, wrapped in ribbon with a bow. As it was being lowered to the ground, she turned to me and said, "But that's the cheapest model." That was her first comment. And thereafter, she never drove it, which, for me, was the best deal in the world because I had a lot of fun taking that sucker out.

ME: What happened when you actually stopped working?

John McAfee: We had cash in the bank and three times as much out there being invested on our behalf. Because Linda had handled all the finances, I had never really paid attention to what we had and where it was. But when I stopped working and finally took a moment to look around and assess where I was positioned, I was very happy to have a super-rich lifestyle from a financial standpoint, without having to live the typical social lifestyle required to partner it.

I think I'm one of the few people who managed to become super-rich and then stop. Can you imagine Bill Gates just walking away when Microsoft was about to explode? Or Richard Branson bailing when Virgin was about to shoot off? Shit, no. They kept working harder. And they did so because they only ever did it for the money, whereas I didn't. Don't get me wrong: I didn't want to give any of it back, but it wasn't my goal to get it in the first place. It just came to me.

To that extent, I was unique, and for me, this was the beginning of a new life instead of me feeling like I was retiring. Although I had never really *worked* in the past, I did at least have to stay in the same city for the duration of each job. And I even pushed the boundaries of that as far as I could. But now, I had no ties at all and more money than I could ever spend.

ME: So, with all of the above in mind, what did you do?

John McAfee: I wasn't exactly happy with Linda, but I knew that if I was to divorce her, I'd most likely be tied up in court for a year and a half. The financial implications didn't concern me; I just didn't want to waste time that I could better use doing something more fun. So I decided to just live with her, and to that extent, I sat her down and said, "Now, listen, you know that I love you dearly and that you'll get half of everything, but I can't live with you permanently anymore. I just can't do it." So, I took our first Mercedes convertible and our dog, Red, and went to Colorado to a house I'd recently started building on the proviso that I'd return to California every two weeks.

ME: How was she about all this?

John McAfee: Initially, she was fine with the arrangement. And in any case, I was trying to accommodate her wishes because, by this time, she was quite happy in this high-flying company she'd been keeping. She liked rubbing shoulders with the super-rich and going to so-called charity fundraisers, and when I was back, I'd put on a tuxedo and go with her now and again. But it just wasn't for me. I despised these *charity* events and saw them only as scams to put more money in the pockets of people who didn't have a clever enough idea of their own to create something.

After a year or so of going back and forth between Colorado and Santa Cruz, I sat her down again and said, "Linda, I can't spend a whole week here once a month. How about I come home for just a weekend every two weeks?" Again, she agreed to that, and that arrangement, in theory, continued until 2004, when we eventually got divorced. It became absurd beyond belief. Everybody knew we weren't a couple. Jesus, I was in newspapers with other women in various parts of the world.

ME: What exactly were you doing in Colorado?

John McAfee: I built this mansion in the mountains of Colorado on four hundred acres, ten miles from the nearest small town, Woodland Park, and forty miles from Colorado Springs. In the winter, I was completely cut off; the house was at an elevation of ten thousand feet at the foot of the Rockies. No town or county was going to come out and clear the access roads. So, I needed snowblowers, snowplows, tractors, forklifts, and generators to clear the roads and to create my own power if I had to. I had a whole hangar full of vehicles for various uses on this remote, beautiful property. I stayed in that house for longer than any other. Although I traveled extensively, I was there for eleven years. I was blissfully happy there.

ME: When and how did you build this property?

John McAfee: I started it during the last years of working at McAfee, and it was as much about the act of building it as it was about actually living there. The whole project took five years, but when I started going down there at that time when I was going back and forth to California, only the first 2,500 square feet was finished. But it was livable, just for me.

And then, while I was living there, it was expanded to the west to include a Frank Lloyd Wright-inspired section. I basically borrowed the block style from his Ennis House in Los Angeles, except that where he had the block constructed by pouring concrete, I had it hand-carved out of sandstone. The edges were crisp and sharp, with none of that concrete bubble. The block alone cost me $7 million, including all the imported artwork that went in it. The entire build process for the mansion cost me in the vicinity of $20 million, not that I ever really ever kept track of anything I spent.

ME: Why not? That sounds crassly irresponsible.

John McAfee: There comes a point where, if you have enough money and investments working for you, you just can't spend it all. I don't say this to belittle the amounts involved or to come across as blasé, but it's just a fact. While I was spending $20 million on a property in Colorado, the interest alone being earned on my money was far in excess of that amount. A money manager was taking care of all that. That's what happens when you reach a certain level of wealth.

And it wasn't just the property I built at Woodland Park. I built a horse farm for six horses, six cabins, two yoga centers, one of which was 6,000 square feet, and a giant shed for all the gear. I had a permanent live-in staff of seven people. It was a colossal undertaking from a maintenance standpoint alone. There were 6,000 electrical outlets with bulbs that needed changing.

ME: What was the attraction of the wilderness kind of lifestyle? It's the diametric opposite of Silicon Valley.

John McAfee: Subconsciously, that was probably the point. Initially, I liked the isolation. I spent most of my time outside, undertaking maintenance work on the property and doing some serious hiking. In the dark winter months, I started lifting weights, writing, and then I started a yoga center and began hosting bespoke yoga retreats. I had thousands of people come through, and most of them I didn't even bother charging. They came, we fed them, and we housed them in cottages on the property for weeks on end. Some never left—quite a few never left. My staff numbers gradually started growing. One part of me was saying, "What the fuck?" The other half of me was saying, "I can't just kick these people out...."

ME: If I'm being honest, this sounds more like a cult. What did you know about yoga?

John McAfee: I can see why. But it really wasn't. It did, however, continue for three years or so. Since a couple of brief trips to India and Nepal in my late twenties that I neglected to mention, I'd always had an interest in yoga and meditation. In Delhi, I learned about transcendental meditation with the Maharishi, the founding yogi of that technique. I discovered yoga, breath work, and meditation. It was exhausting and also enlightening.

When I came back, my hair was shoulder-length, and I had cultivated a goatee beard. I was a proto-hippie, just respectable enough to keep getting jobs in technology and just cool enough to mix it with any sort of hippie crew. When the Maharishi started his movement across the US in the late '70s, I continued dabbling, depending on where I was living/working at that time.

ME: I've been talking to you long enough and think I know you well enough to call you out here. This yoga center concept, in combination with people staying on the property permanently, doesn't make any sense. What was the deal?

John McAfee: OK. Let me be honest here. The real reason I started the yoga retreat was to get women. And given that it was mostly women who were interested in yoga retreats, it seemed like a logical way. Not just that, because they were interested in doing yoga, chances are they were bright, healthy, and in good shape.

ME: I have to say this sounds like cynical behavior at best.

John McAfee: What was the alternative? The nearest town had a gas station, two restaurants, a bank, and a small rodeo arena. There were certainly no young women that I'd have been interested in there, and I wasn't exactly going to drive forty miles to Colorado Springs just to get laid. I was two hundred miles away from fucking Denver! So I thought, *I'll just bring them here. That solves all my pussy problems.* And so, that was the plan.

Inevitably, the ones who stayed were the women; it inevitably became a bit of a sex paradise at the beginning. But once I'd been doing this for a couple of years, with two or three new ones staying on each visit, the social tension among these women became palpable. When we were doing yoga, just the girls and me, you could slice the tension in that fucking room with a knife.

ME: It's not exactly polygamy, but it sounds a bit like it.

John McAfee: I need to make it clear. This was not a scam. I had been to India and meditated with the Maharishi. I could teach yoga and had studied it for years. I could do any pose; when people came, they learned. But I didn't do it all out of the kindness of my heart to spread love and peace. Nor was I doing it because I enjoyed yoga that much myself. As much as I was a master of it, there were plenty of other things I'd have rather been doing. No, I did it for one reason and one reason only: to fuck many women without ever having to leave my property. But, after a while, I sensed that familiar feeling of impending doom.

I had to shut the whole thing down. I could see that I was creating a potentially uncontrollable monster right on my own doorstep. My yoga retreats succeeded and failed simultaneously. And in the long run, the whole thing probably cost me a million bucks all told, given that I had to feed all these people, etc. There was no investment lost. I still owned everything after the people left; I wrote four books on yoga in the long winter months.

However, the local town of Woodland Park did benefit from my running these retreats. Several people moved there from other areas. It is one of the most beautiful places, right on the slopes of the Rocky Mountains, with uninterrupted views of Pikes Peak—all 14,115 feet of it.

ME: Why did you write those yoga books and then publicly trash them?

John McAfee: Because they were nothing but naïve garbage. They weren't inaccurate per se, but the only one I read after it was published, *Into the Heart of Truth*, confused even me. As I read it, I was thinking, *What's he talking about?*

ME: Sure, but you wrote them and must have thought they were worthy at the time. Why the need to actively distance yourself from them and sabotage sales?

John McAfee: I probably did think they were serviceable at the time. And, in any case, I only wrote them to fill my evenings when it was dark at 5 p.m., and there was nothing else going on. I didn't have cable, and I got tired of watching movies, so I just cranked four books out one after another. But I later criticized them because I didn't want people to read them. I was embarrassed to have written them and to have regurgitated so much of what I'd read so many times over the years. What does it matter?

ME: It matters because it makes you look impulsive and unpredictable. And apart from anything else, what will you later say about this book?

John McAfee: I am impulsive and unpredictable, so it wasn't as if my criticizing these books should have come as a surprise to anyone. With this book, I trust you to portray me fairly.

ME: Did any of the women you met at the yoga retreats stay in your life afterward?

John McAfee: Yes, actually. Jennifer, her name was. She came for one of the courses and just stayed. She became my girlfriend, and by 2002, I had divorced Linda because she wanted to go off and remarry, which I was perfectly fine with.

ME: When did you get started on the whole idea of aero-trekking/sport flying?

John McAfee: After the yoga center closed down, I found myself looking out of the window, admiring what was around me. The house was finished—as finished as a place like that was ever likely to be—and the views to Pikes Peak were just breathtaking. I had various women friends who liked to come and go hiking with Jennifer and me, one of whom was Grace Jones' sister, Pam, who lived in Colorado Springs at the time. She would come up with her friend, and they'd hike, maybe spend the night; it was all just fine.

Then I thought to myself, *What could I do to broaden the experience of this place?* I desperately wanted to do something beyond just appealing to various parasitic friends who wanted to come in from out of state and women, many of whom just wanted to move in with me.

I started getting enthused by the idea of flying these micro-light type aircraft with single airplane engines, which allowed you to skim just a few feet above the ground. There was an incredible sense of freedom attached to what is called sport flying over wheat fields at a height where you could almost touch the crop with your bare feet, or flying below telephone wires at ninety miles per hour instead of above them. Sometimes I'd put a slow wing on and go up early in the morning when the air was calm and fly at twenty miles an hour. Before you know it, you are one mile in the air and looking at the Earth from a hawk's perspective. And hawks, by the way, were my best friends. Birds in general don't like these slow wings. It freaks them out; they fly away. But hawks will seek you out. They'll soar right off your wing, looking at you as if to say, "What the fuck are you? How are you even flying?" Then they'll soar with you for thirty seconds and then reappear on the other wing.

Now, this all might not *sound* so great. But sex itself doesn't sound great until you've actually done it. But believe me, sport flying was intoxicating in its appeal for me. Typical of me, I dived into this pursuit headfirst.

ME: In what sense? What was your broader vision for where this sport could go?

John McAfee: Once I realized that flying was something I wanted to do as a passion, I also acknowledged that the only suitable places that this could be safely done were in the vast expanses of wilderness in the Southwest, in states like Arizona, New Mexico, and Utah—far away from inconveniences like highways, pylons, and electricity lines. So what I decided on was to create a network of landing strips whereby someone could fly all day over the wilderness.

To do that, what I did was drive around with Jennifer in a Hummer, and we spent many weeks camping and identifying places where I could build these airstrips. For a few years, this sport consumed me. It was my whole life. I had two airstrips at my own house and a hangar full of planes. I ended up getting four out of the ten I'd planned built, and then my nephew Joel died. And when that happened, I canned everything.

ME: Was it simply an accident?

John McAfee: It was. We don't even know what really happened. He was in the remote wilderness, and he had a passenger. All that we know is that they crashed into the side of a mountain and were both killed.

ME: Did you blame yourself?

John McAfee: Not for the crash itself. That was truly an accident. But I did have an awareness that this activity I had created with sport flying was probably one of the most inherently dangerous sports out there.

ME: You had to fend off a wrongful death lawsuit, right?

John McAfee: In fact, the lawyers, when they sued me, claimed that it was, statistically speaking, the most dangerous sport in the world. Maybe that was just lawyer talk. I don't know. But because I'd lost my nephew Joel, who had become kind of a son to me, even I realized that I had lost him because I had crossed the line of risk acceptability. I took risks that no sane man should have ever taken. I personally only survived because of sheer luck. I was in so many tight situations where I had no clue how I escaped. And yet I did. Joel was only twenty-one. How could he have understood how to calculate risk? He didn't know shit about danger. He just saw me, his uncle, doing it, and so, he wanted to do it too.

Others wanted to continue, and I said, "Go ahead. You know what the risks are now." I left my planes there and never went back until I auctioned everything off a couple of years later.

ME: Was this what made you leave for Belize? Did you flee to avoid the repercussions of the lawsuit?

John McAfee: Well, I didn't leave for legal reasons. It was an indescribable tragedy to lose Joel and a wrench to have to walk away from my passion. But I wasn't wrestling with the decision or forcing myself to leave. I just knew that leaving was something that had to happen. I'm never one to deliberate about things for too long. No, in such situations, I just calmly ask myself, "What is it that needs to happen now?" And what had to happen was for me to get a total change of perspective because everything in Colorado—the house, the planes, etc.—reminded me of Joel. I didn't leave for legal reasons.

ME: Was this when you went to Belize?

JOHN MCAFEE: Not quite. In 2006, after Joel's death, I was certainly thinking about leaving, but Jennifer and I hadn't yet decided where we wanted to go. However, I had business to attend to before I left.

I had to get rid of everything in Colorado. I also had other properties scattered around that I'd either built, or had built, over the preceding few years. I should probably tell you about those.

ME: Why did you build these places in the first place? Just because you could?

JOHN MCAFEE: Partly that, I suppose. I like the process of conceiving an idea and seeing it through. While living in Colorado, I had traveled all over the world and been inspired by different places, their architecture and their art. I enjoy sourcing materials and incorporating them all into a design that was totally unique. I just like constructing buildings to an extremely high level of quality. Some of them obviously had some kind of attraction as a place to live permanently. But inevitably, because my life is so complex and I travel around a lot, there are a few houses that I built spending many millions of dollars that I never actually lived in.

One such example is a house I built in South Padre Island in Texas. Flat, hot; I have no idea why people want to live there, but at some point, I thought I did because the fishing was good. So I built a mansion that was essentially three mansions in one, right on the ocean. And all three were three levels high and were interconnected by external stairways in the style of the Dutch artist M.C. Escher. You'd have a stairway going from level three of house one to level two of house two. Then another stairway from level one of house two going to level three of house three and so on. It was so confusing that people staying there would occasionally need rescuing. I only set foot in it three times in total.

ME: You need to explain. That sounds completely ludicrous.

John McAfee: I always had people project managing these builds for me. There were a few of them over the years, but the best of them was a woman called Maria, who I met with her now-boyfriend at the yoga retreat in Colorado. She lived with me briefly in the house before Jennifer came on the scene. We had an affair. I loved her at the time. Very smart woman.

So, whenever I found a location in which I wanted to build a property, the first thing I did was call Maria. And from there, she'd take over all the logistics of liaising with architects and contractors with a view to getting it built. All the time, we'd be talking on the phone, and she'd be updating me on progress. And then, once it was built and the house was secured and staffed, she moved on to the next place with me.

ME: So you're telling me that you built this house, spent millions on it, staffed it, and then it just sat there? And you spent three nights in it total? That sounds implausible.

John McAfee: It was possibly only two nights, when I think about it. When it was built, I didn't actually care for the place very much. It was a very complicated relationship I had with that house. So, yes, I was there for a couple of days, and then I decided I wanted to go and look at a piece of land in Hawaii.

Now, I'd always loved Hawaii. I loved the food, the people, the culture—everything. When I was still with Linda, we regularly went there, and rather than build something in Hawaii, I leased the presidential suite at the Royal Hawaiian Hotel, The Pink Palace, in Honolulu for an entire year a time. This would have been during that period when I was traveling back and forth from Colorado.

We had all the furniture swapped out for things we liked, and then we just went down there whenever we felt like it. It was like a home away from home. And when we arrived, it was like something out of the fucking old movies, with all the hotel staff lined up outside to greet us as we got out of the limousine. Soon I knew all the staff by name, and whenever I arrived, I tipped every one of them $1,000, except for the concierge, who got five. The whole staff was my staff. I kept the lease going for several years until it became too dangerous to go to Hawaii.

ME: What do you mean it became too dangerous to go to Hawaii?

JOHN MCAFEE: Having spent time in Hawaii, I ultimately bought two houses in Hawaii at various times. But the one that was problematic was in Molokai, which is a small island populated almost exclusively by natives. I had no interest in the island itself. There were no tourist services. There was nothing there for gringos whatsoever. The natives were less than friendly.

We discovered Molokai on a whale-watching boat trip from Maui, and while we were out there, this pod of humpback whales appeared a mile off-shore from Molokai. One of them came right up to the boat and just sat there. We could touch it. The boat captain said he'd never seen anything like it in twenty years of running whale-watching tours. That experience deeply touched me, and so, I wanted to dock at Molokai to have a look around. In that moment, I thought, *That was a sign....*

ME: So you bought a house because of that event?

JOHN MCAFEE: To cut a long story short, yes. We found a realtor who took us around, and we bought this beautiful property on the east end of the island, a real nice place on a cliff above the beach. I bought it from a white guy from California who'd built it years previously and never lived there because people just aren't welcoming to outsiders. Then I went to the west end of the island and bought ten acres of the most dramatic piece of seascape you have ever seen, where the waves break over the volcanic rock and the spray shoots up a hundred feet in the air. It was spectacular. Then began a six-year project to build a house that I never once set foot in.

ME: But you completed this place? I'm struggling to grasp the point of this on two levels. One, why spend six years building a house in a place where you're not welcome? And two, why build a place and never set foot in it? People will not be able to comprehend this.

John McAfee: Yes, it was finished. I sold it when I went to Belize. Maria used to call me all the time and say, "You've got to come and see this house!" But by that time, I was in Ecuador building the largest condo in the entire country. I had lost all interest in Hawaii. This would have been 2004 or 2005.

ME: You said things went bad in Hawaii? In what way?

John McAfee: Holy fuck, things went sideways. There are a few things out there online about it, but none of them are the truth.

I liked Molokai, and I actually spent a bit of time in the first ready-built house I had bought while I was planning the build of the second one on the seascape land. But the reason I got into trouble in Molokai was that, while I was there, I realized that Molokai had one of the highest rates of methamphetamine use anywhere in America—albeit none of the natives even considered themselves to be American citizens. Seriously, I would see kids literally starving at the roadside while their parents were strung out on drugs and missing teeth, etc. It was tragic, and, of course, by this time, having been clean for almost twenty years, I'd gone full circle and become something of a drug sheriff.

ME: Did you meddle in the workings of this island community?

John McAfee: I wanted to make things better, let's put it that way. I contacted this former drug addict who was working with addicts, and I asked this guy to take me around and show me where all the meth houses were on the island. We took a professional photographer with us to document all of this. Some of these places were beside schools; others were near churches. I then took out full-page ads in Hawaii's largest newspapers and put one of these photographs alongside a headline that read something like, "This is a meth house beside a grade school. Why are you allowing this?" Well, this really embarrassed the governor, who, along with the police, chose to turn a blind eye to Molokai's drug problems, simply because it was the last remaining real native island, and it was always politically sensitive to meddle in its affairs.

ME: Did the embarrassment lead to action by the police and governor?

John McAfee: It was all a tactical error on my behalf. I thought I was helping and being smart. But the police swooped in and flushed every fucking trace of drugs out of Molokai. Every meth house was gone within six months.

ME: Wasn't that a good thing?

John McAfee: In isolation, yes. But the drugs business brought in money. Money paid for food. Suddenly, there was none of either. And I, the gringo, was blamed for that. To say that I became persona non grata in Molokai would be an understatement, even though the road to hell is paved with good intentions, as the saying goes.

My life then took an ugly fucking turn because I needed the natives to sign the permits that would allow me to build on some sacred land on the island I'd also purchased. I'd barely squeaked by on the work I did on the existing property, and that was before I shut down the drug trade. I knew I was going to get nothing from them, so I made my next big mistake, which was to fly an American company in to auction the land off.

Now, that's not the sort of thing you can just do in Hawaii. I should have sensed impending doom. Natives don't view land ownership like we gringos do. To cut a long story short, it became this ugly showdown between the locals and me, and we had to bring in local riot police on the day of the auction, in addition to five FBI agents. Bloodshed was expected. There were three hundred people there with machetes shouting, "Carve him up. Carve him up," as I stood behind a cordon of police. It ended up in a near-riot; nobody was killed. But the auction went ahead nevertheless. That was the last day I ever spent in Hawaii. I sold the first house I bought remotely years later when I was in Belize.

ME: Do you regret what you tried to do in Hawaii?

John McAfee: I brought everything upon myself through a combination of arrogance and stupidity. I was a white man who knew jack shit about Hawaiian culture really, even though I'd been going there for years. All I knew was the Pink Palace and that everything was plastic. In reality, I knew nothing about the culture on Molokai, the last real Hawaiian island. What the fuck was I thinking?

ME: To me, there are obvious parallels between what happened in Molokai and what later happened in Belize? It's impossible for me to ignore that connection. It feels like you have a messiah complex.

John McAfee: Yeah, OK. I admit I have a fault. I do look at situations and think that they can be fixed. But the reality is that it's not that simple. Because if it was, none of the socio-economic problems that we have in the world today would exist. Life is just not that simple, as much as I wish it was. I never learned. If someone took all the children off the Earth, it would be so much easier for me. I just can't stand children suffering because their parents are whacked out on drugs. I go crazy, and I do stupid shit, and what I gradually found out was that the police in these places were usually the ones benefitting most from the drug trade anyway.

ME: You won't like this, but I'm going to ask you anyway: why do you care about the children of Belize and Molokai so much when you barely have a relationship with any of your own?

John McAfee: That's not the same.

ME: I'd say it is. They are your kids, aren't they?

John McAfee: Yes, but they are not living in poverty as far as I'm aware, and in some cases, the women whose children I had never even told me about the kids anyway, and therefore, I was never involved in their lives directly after they were born. Regrettably, I do not have a very good relationship with my daughter, though. We talk, but not often.

ME: Why did you choose Ecuador to build?

JOHN MCAFEE: I'd grown tired of physically roaming around discovering new places. I'd gotten lazy and, at the same time, started realizing there were internet sites available for idiots like me who were just looking for the next new and glamorous place to live or own property.

I started searching for the best places to live on the planet, and I started noticing that Cuenca, Ecuador, appeared on almost every top ten list. It was known as "The City of Perpetual Spring" because, although it sits directly on the equator, because it's at an elevation of 9,000 feet, the climate is perfect year-round. Nobody needed air conditioning; nobody needed heat. You didn't need jack shit.

I settled on Cuenca in which to build a house in the mountains, but when I started talking to locals in the know, they told me, "It'll be a twenty-five-year process. That's just the way it works." As a compromise, I decided to build a seventeen-story condo in the city, which would become the most expensive building in all of Ecuador when complete. In advance, I purchased the top floor of the building for myself. I have no idea how many millions I put into all of that.

ME: Would I be right in saying that, as South American countries go, Ecuador would be one of the more civilized?

JOHN MCAFEE: There are no civilized South American countries, my friend. It is where Edward Snowden and Julian Assange wanted to go. Let's just say they will tolerate rich white men. That's the best I can say about Ecuador. But I only ever went there twice and for a total of six days. Meanwhile, my business advisor, Maria, was living down there. She fell in love with Cuenca, and I rented her a place to live in while the condo was being built. Again, she managed the whole thing. I was still madly in love with her, and in many ways, I still am.

ME: Looking back at all this, what were you trying to achieve with all of this extravagant building?

John McAfee: I saw it all like art or sculpture. I wanted to create something beautiful. The process of creating it was what I enjoyed. But did I want to live in my art? Hell no. I lived in the Colorado house, but in my eyes, it was the ugliest house I ever built. Its functionality far exceeded its artistic value, albeit that when most people walked into it for the first time, they almost fainted because of the grandeur. But Colorado paled in significance relative to other places I built in Texas, Ecuador, New Mexico, Tucson, and Hawaii. So, yes, it was *only* about the process. Once I'd built these places, my need for them disappeared.

ME: At what point did you sell all your possessions in the US?

John McAfee: Shortly before leaving for Belize in 2008, I organized what amounted to a giant yard sale at my mansion in Colorado. Everything went in it. Houses, cabins, dozens of cars, Airstream trailers, machinery, and valuable art and decor—every fucking thing I owned was available to be purchased and taken away. Some of it I let people take away for nothing. People came from the surrounding towns and cities and basically picked the place clean. The house itself was sold to a from Chicago. It went for $5 million. He got a great deal. Then later, once I was in Belize, the various other houses in New Mexico, Tucson, Texas, etc. were all sold at auction also, with all the various items related to sport flying that went with them. These properties sold, but because of the 2008 financial crisis, the prices I got were far less than they might have been a few years earlier. But I honestly didn't care.

By that point, I just wanted closure of everything. Joel's death had been the catalyst, and, from that standpoint, selling everything was easy because pretty much everything I had in the US just reminded me of him. Beyond that, I realized that having multiple properties scattered all over the world was completely impractical. I just wanted to draw a line under everything and to make a clean start in a new place. At no point did I feel like I had lost anything. Have you ever lost someone dear to you, Mark? Someone in your family?

ME: My father died fifteen years ago.

John McAfee: If you had the choice to give away every material position you had in exchange for him living another ten or twenty years, I bet you would do it, right?

ME: Of course.

John McAfee: That's how I felt when I got rid of everything. I just wish I could have brought Joel back in exchange.

NINE

HEART OF DARKNESS

A few days before my next call with McAfee, I watched the documentary entitled *Gringo: The Dangerous Life of John McAfee* on Netflix, and I have to confess that I found it to be confusing viewing. It's not for me to say what the filmmakers' motives were, but the conclusion I reached after watching the film was that they wanted to present McAfee not just as a deranged murderer but also as a calculating rapist.

By any standards, these were very serious allegations that, although unsubstantiated, nevertheless made me feel quite uncomfortable about my relationship with him, even though there was a degree of mutual trust, and everything seemed genuine. But what made things even more difficult was that some of the testimonies in the film were from people that McAfee had and would reference again—people who were dear to him.

To that extent, rumors that some of these people had been bribed by the filmmakers to say certain things for the purposes of the documentary's revelatory angle seemed plausible. Belize was, after all, a pretty lawless place by all accounts, where money was tight for many and bribes were commonplace.

Certain things about the documentary just didn't add up, though. Equally, I was perfectly willing to go into our conversations about what happened down in Belize expecting that McAfee's version of events might not add up either. I was objective enough about it all to know that, in circumstances whereby saying something might put him in serious trouble, McAfee might well omit certain information or flat out lie. I was on guard for any change in tone or mannerisms that might suggest we were entering into touchy territory.

ME: How does a person start living in a country like Belize?

John McAfee: I went online in early 2007, looked at all the houses for sale, picked one, called the realtor, and sent the money. I never set foot in the house before buying it. It was a risk, just like anything else.

ME: As someone who pays so much attention to detail when building houses, it seems strange to just buy a place blind off the internet.

John McAfee: I didn't want to spend a week down there with fucking realtors being shown around. Later that year, we went down there for the first time. Jennifer loved the place; I double loved the place. The house was perfect—a "pod" design with a central area with the living room, dining room, and kitchen in the middle. This was a massive area, with windows on all sides, right on the beach on the southern end of Ambergris quay. There were various other bedrooms, all in effect separate houses situated close by but connected to the main building by covered walkways. From every front room, you could see the beach and the reef a quarter of a mile offshore.

ME: So when did you go down to live in Belize full-time?

sJohn McAfee: Nothing for me is ever completely full-time, but for the purposes of the question, let's say I was in Belize for most of my time from about 2008 onwards until I had to leave in 2012. When I got down there with Jennifer, I did what I normally did somewhere new: I assembled my toys, the specific items I'd need to make life fun in the new environment I was going into. In Santa Cruz, it was cars. In Colorado, off-road vehicles, etc.

In Belize, given that everything revolved around the ocean and fishing, I was going to need a good boat. So I had a thirty-two-foot boat made for me by Bradley Boat Works, which was basically just one man. Two engines on the back, very fast; it was a lot of fun. And then I bought a forty-four-foot catamaran, a workboat for the staff to use to get to town, and a couple of jet skis.

ME: It has been rumored widely that you lost all your money in the 2008 financial crisis. Is there any truth in that?

John McAfee: The market crash never impacted my finances. I was always an extremely conservative investor. Morgan Stanley were my money managers and my orders were pretty much the same all the time. I didn't want ten per cent; I didn't even want five per cent. My attitude was "I want one per cent. But just don't lose my fucking money." And they didn't. I was in triple 'A' rated bonds throughout the whole stock market crash.

ME: Where exactly was your house in Belize?

John McAfee: The town of San Pedro, where my beach house was located, was touristy, white, and populated mostly by wealthy Americans, many of whom came down for vacations or to spend six months of the year, etc. To that extent, I fit in just fine there. People liked me. I quickly became part of the community, and Jennifer soon opened and was running a nice little coffee shop called The Sail Away Café, which quickly became one of San Pedro's most frequented landmarks.

ME: Was there any specific agenda down there, or did you see this as retirement?

John McAfee: I honestly hadn't even thought about it. I was just going with the flow, kicking back, and, for the first couple of years, I just sailed around on my boat, went to the outer islands, explored the reef, and generally had a fine time in what was essentially paradise. Then that got boring, and at that point, I started looking around for shit to do.

ME: Before you explain what that entailed, can you give me a sense of what Belize is like?

JOHN MCAFEE: The natives are primarily black, and the primary language is English, albeit not everyone speaks it very well. The real language is Belizean Creole, which is a simplification of English, and then, thereafter, Spanish is the second language. The country was formerly British Honduras until the colonialists left in 1981, in turn leaving the country in the hands of largely uneducated people. You can, therefore, probably imagine what kind of governments were going to spring up.

By the time I showed up down there, the Belizean prime minister, Dean Barrow, had not only had the country's military at his command, but also his own private army on call—the "gang suppression unit" he called it—most of whom were little more than street thugs.

Meanwhile, among the general population, there was palpable and festering anger from hundreds of years of British rule. There was genuine racial hatred in the air at all times, and I knew all that from very early on in my time in Belize.

ME: What "shit" did you find to do?

JOHN MCAFEE: The first thing I do when I get to a new place is look around and see what's missing. To that end, after a couple of months, I noticed that the ferry system that serviced the island—Island Ferries—really wasn't very efficient. They had a few open boats that held fifty or so people, and these ferries moved people up and down the coast of San Pedro, which was about forty miles from one end to the other. There were schedules for when and where they were supposed to pick people up, and one of the stops was the dock of my house.

Well, these boats were routinely showing up an hour late. Not just that, they only ran four boats per day. So I started my own ferry company called Coastal Express and bought a fleet of high-capacity boats and painted them red. We ran every half hour. When our schedule said we'd be at a certain dock at 2:15 p.m., we were there.

ME: Why did you do this?

John McAfee: Good question. It wasn't for the money, that's for fucking sure. No white man was ever going to make any money in Belize. But they didn't mind people building shit, especially if it benefitted local people. And I guess, from my side, you could say that I was just being benevolent in a subconscious attempt to ingratiate myself with the locals. As if to prove it, I hired only local people, unlike every other business in San Pedro, who only ever employed white people, which I always thought was so fucking stupid.

ME: On paper, you were simply improving things by investing in the town where you were living.

John McAfee: I was, but within two months, I'd put Island Ferries out of business in spectacular fashion. I ended up buying them out (gave the guy a good price too), taking their boats, and painting them all red. In no time at all, I had created an efficient ferry company that not only serviced the island properly but also gave the locals jobs. What could possibly go fucking wrong?

ME: What did go wrong?

John McAfee: Well, let's see. One of my boats killed a tourist by running over this guy, at night, at least a hundred yards from shore. Who the fuck swims at night, that far from shore? Nevertheless, that happened, drew lawsuits, and caused all kinds of friction. Someone else got their leg amputated by a propeller during the day while they were snorkeling. They came up underneath the boat apparently.

Then there were all kinds of personnel issues to contend with: people not showing up, people fighting, or being drunk. Finally, I hired a friend, Eddie Ancona, to run the whole thing on my behalf. I just couldn't deal with the nuances of Belizean pecking orders, etc. After a bit longer, when the business needed for nothing, I washed my hands of it altogether and signed the whole thing over to the workers collectively as a gift. It's still running now. If you go to Belize, the Coastal Express water taxis are still going up and down the coast, probably on the same schedules.

ME: Do you think that, as much as you were improving the infrastructure, there was resistance to you from the government? Were they thinking, "Who does this guy think he is?"

John McAfee: In San Pedro, nobody gave a shit. They just wanted a ferry. And I forgot to say that locals paid half the price that tourists did. Also, I instituted a policy whereby all school children rode for free during the school year. I never made a dime from any Belizean business while I was there, nor did I ever anticipate making one. The locals were fine with it, but I don't think the government and its associated thugs up in Belize City liked what I was doing at all, as I'd soon find out.

Everything was fine. For a couple of years, I was this happy-go-lucky dude. We could easily have stayed there and lived a quiet life by the beach, and still been there now. But San Pedro, for all its beach appeal, wasn't the real Belize, and I've always been searching for *real*. I've been seeking it my whole life one way or another. But to find it in Belize, I had to head inland, to a foreboding interior area called Orange Walk, whose main center of population, Orange Walk Town, lies at the northern end of the district.

ME: What did you want to do there?

John McAfee: I suppose, as mad as it now sounds, I thought I could build a jungle house by the New River and live in harmony with the natives, all of whom were black and many of whom shared their government's fundamental mistrust of wealthy white men like me. Part of me, I suppose, also wanted to test myself in a raw, untamed environment that exposed humanity in a way that a sanitized, white beach resort just couldn't.

ME: Given what had happened in Hawaii, was this a wise policy?

John McAfee: Probably not. And when I talked to my best Belizean friend, Eddie Ancona, a carpenter I'd hired shortly after arriving in Belize to change the woodwork in the beach house in San Pedro, he said, "That's really not a good idea."

I trusted Eddie, and Jennifer and I became friendly with him and his wife, who were both fundamental Christians. Eddie worked on my beach house for over a year. In addition to changing the woodwork, he also fitted wall-to-wall bookcases. He was a really skilled and diligent craftsman who never once wore shoes, and what I gave him was probably a job of a lifetime from a financial perspective.

But, of course, I didn't fucking listen to Eddie. No, I was stupid enough and arrogant enough to think that somehow, I could make such a ludicrous situation work. So we flew over there, Jennifer, Eddie, and me. This must have been sometime in 2010, shortly after I took a boat trip up the jungle river and found myself spellbound by the sheer rawness of the environment and the Mayan ruins that lay hidden in the jungle's darkest corners.

Anyway, we found this property on two acres beside the New River on a low-lying piece of ground that looked as if it needed to be raised to avoid being flooded when the New River ran high in periods of heavy rain. I was sold on this place. Jennifer was not.

While we were in Orange Walk, Eddie introduced me to all the main players, including...whoa.... Do I have to talk about this?

ME: Including whom?

John McAfee: I'm not sure how wise it is for me to name names like this....

ME: Why not?

John McAfee: These are dangerous people. We may need to review this later. Anyway, the man I was going to mention was Rodwell Richards, who everybody knew was the most feared hit man in Central America. He had a staff that consisted of ex-Belizean Defense Force psychos, and he just took hit jobs on behalf of mostly the prime minister, Dean Barrow, and sometimes for other cabinet ministers. Eddie introduced me to all the major players who would assist with transforming my life in Belize from being laid-back and keeping myself to myself to being a man in constant conflict with a violent entity who insisted that I toe the line at all times.

ME: It sounds like you brought all this on yourself. You were warned, but you ignored that warning.

JOHN MCAFEE: Eddie did warn me, but he was never forceful about it. He just said, "You are going to need security," which I knew. But it wouldn't have mattered what he said at that point. I had made my mind up I was going to the jungle, and nobody could persuade me otherwise.

I bought the land we'd seen on the initial foray into the jungle, and on my next trip there, I went up to the nearest township to seek out people to work on building the house and the various other cottages that I wanted on the land. As I walked through the streets on my way to meet the local natives known as Mennonites who I was going to employ to do the construction, all I heard was, "Hey white man!" being shouted from windows as I walked by.

ME: You were just reenacting *Heart of Darkness*, weren't you?

JOHN MCAFEE: Nonsense, this wasn't *Heart of Darkness* at all. That was a novel about a psychosis that turned dark. This was just me and the jungle, with a bunch of locals who were initially very friendly.

You have to see and come into contact with something before you can truly hate it, right? Yes, they had seen white people; there were tourist boat trips now and again up the New River from Orange Walk Town to the Mayan ruins I mentioned at Lamanai.

But they had never seen a white person in the circumstances under which I was showing up: walking into the jungle and building a house among them or walking into Paz Novella's strip club, Lover's Bar, to sit at night and watch the girls dance, or showing up at the local market at dawn on a Sunday morning to see if I could get some fresh fucking tomatoes, or at the local food court where the poor ate because you could get a good meal for next to nothing. No white person had ever done any of these things. But I did. Pretty soon, after the initial shock and novelty had worn off, they realized I was just a harmless old man who was fundamentally nice and generous. I started wandering into Orange Walk to fraternize with the locals, especially the women.

ME: Ah, yes. Inevitably there were women involved....

John McAfee: You should know this by now. However, in order to understand the women I was involved with in Belize, you first have to understand Mr. Pazus Novella. He owned and ran a club called Lover's Bar in Orange Walk Town, which was basically a front for prostitution, which, by the way, is perfectly legal and accepted in Belize. Pazus was my friend and, simultaneously, my enemy. In his capacity as second cousin to Gaspar Vega, the assistant prime minister at the time, Paz tried to have me collected and killed as many times as anybody.

At the beginning, however, when I first arrived in the jungle, I had said to my assistant, "Where are all the women?" "Lover's," he told me. I went to Lover's one afternoon and bought everyone a beer, including the Mennonites, who weren't even supposed to drink and fuck women but did anyway. I didn't even talk to anyone. Then, the next day, I did the same thing: I bought everybody a beer. By this point, girls were trying to climb on me.

ME: What was your angle by doing this?

John McAfee: I was just paying close fucking attention because I wanted to identify these women and their characteristics. And very quickly, I identified the ones who would both steal your wallet and slash your throat so that you couldn't tell anybody. There were certainly a few of those. After a while, I had identified four who I thought were 99 percent trustworthy and who were smart enough to realize that by being nice to me, they'd get a lot more money than they would by stealing whatever was in my pocket that day. The first one I met was Tamisha. She was the first girl I took back to my house on the river. She was the first Belizean girl I ever talked to properly.

ME: What happened to Jennifer?

John McAfee: Much like every woman who has ever gone anywhere with me, Jennifer eventually left and went back to the US. And she did this because she finally realized that the reason I was staying away so much in the jungle was that I was seeing many other women all the time.

However, Tamisha's story was tragic. She was a prostitute, maybe twenty years old. She had a daughter, but the daughter's father took her, legally, when she was a baby, and Tamisha was only allowed to see her under supervision. But the father had a girlfriend who was seriously fucking whacked, and she would do things like burn the kid with a fucking iron to the point that she had iron-shaped blisters on her back. She was in this terrible situation. Tamisha knew her daughter was being abused, but because she was in a cycle of prostitution, she couldn't get her back. Her whole psyche was damaged, so I took her in to try and help.

The other girl I started seeing in the earlier days was Amy. These two girls and some others were living with me; we'd go places together, to resorts in the area and even further afield to Mexico, which turned a few heads given I was this smartly dressed, suntanned older white guy with young black girls in tow, often in various states of inappropriate dress. People had never seen that before.

Of course, I was having sex with them all, which was freaky for everybody in retrospect. This is just how it was. I was just doing what I always did. For a while, everything was fine. These women came to me, and they all came via Pazus. I bought their freedom from him with cash, but in turn, they became dependent on me, which was arguably worse.

ME: So what changed?

John McAfee: A couple of things in combination. In 2009, my old college in Roanoke had decided to give me an honorary doctorate. A year or two so later, after I'd moved to the jungle, somebody in Orange Walk Town must have got hold of an old newspaper article that described me as "Dr. McAfee," and the next thing I know, everybody in Orange Walk is saying, "Oh, so he's a doctor?" That was the first problem.

ME: In what sense was it a problem?

John McAfee: Well, not only did they have a white man in the sprawling compound I'd built in their midst, but this white man was also a doctor. Mothers started showing up at my front gate. "Can I talk to Dr. McAfee?" they'd say to my security guards. Out of courtesy, I'd always go down and talk, and the first one who arrived had a baby with her, who was clearly starving: the belly was swollen, the skin was blotched, and the hair was falling out. This infant couldn't have been more than fifteen months old. "Dr. McAfee, can you tell me what's wrong with my child?" she said. "Well, I'm not really that kind of doctor, I'm afraid."

By this point, I told Amy, who was living with me, to go down to the store and buy this woman some beans, rice, meats, and vegetables, and then to unload these provisions at her home. Well, thereafter, an endless stream of women started appearing at my gate.

Eventually, I decided to go into the local village, a place called Carmelita. When I got there, I was shocked by what I saw. I had never seen such poverty. People were living in broken-down cinder-block shacks with no roof. Kids were starving everywhere. So I met with the village elders; they had a school there. But the kids didn't get lunch at school. If lunch had been available, all the adults would have been there too.

So, to cut a long story short, I built a school cafeteria and developed a lunch program that provided food, a refrigerated kitchen, etc., not just for the kids in Carmelita but also for everyone from the surrounding villages to come there. Although they invariably came to me for other things, mothers at least stopped bringing their starving kids to my gate. On balance, I thought I'd solved a major local problem. But it was a real embarrassment for the government.

ME: What was the problem? You had the means to help, and you did.

JOHN MCAFEE: That's how you and I might see it, but that's not how they saw it. People had been starving forever in Orange Walk, and the government had never fixed the problem. Then a white man comes in, and all the food problems are solved. Had I been black, it still might have been a mild affront to the government. But I was white, and the government, as I said, did not like white people. Prime Minister Dean Barrow must have been thinking, *What's a white man doing feeding my people?*

That was the last straw. Wait...actually, it wasn't quite the final last straw.

ME: What was?

JOHN MCAFEE: Let me start by saying that the entirety of the government was corrupt. I'll begin with the least dangerous names and work upwards. The minister of national defense was the biggest drug dealer in the country. The minister for immigration was the largest human trafficker in all of Central America. The minister of finance filled his pockets by selling Belizean passports to Muslims who wanted to access America via Mexico. They could get right to the border on a Belizean passport, and a good proportion would get escorted across in the absence of the wall that I'm glad President Trump has not yet built. For the record, I hope he never does. The assistant prime minister, the second most powerful man in Belize and a more brutal man than the prime minister, ran all the drugs in Orange Walk. His name was Gaspar Vega, and he lived in Orange Walk Town, which was seven miles from where I was living.

ME: I'm assuming that he was uncomfortable with your presence?

JOHN MCAFEE: Not only that. Because of my relationships with the various girls who were coming and going from the compound, I also had started to get an understanding that almost all of Orange Walk's social problems were a result of the drug gangs that Gaspar Vega was in cahoots with. I decided I wanted to clean that shit up for the good of the local people. Because of my relationships with these young girls, I was now invested in a way Mr. Vega didn't want me to be.

ME: Surely you must have felt impending doom? You were about to do exactly what you have done in Molokai, only in an arguably much more dangerous place.

John McAfee: This is all true. A few things were going on at the time, not least that Amy, one of the girls who was living with me at that time, was starting to get extremely unpredictable. If you go online and find the Dateline NBC documentary called *Trouble in Paradise* about my time in Belize, you'll see her on there, calmly admitting that she tried to kill me. She is quite a performer, believe you me.

ME: Why did she want to kill you?

John McAfee: Jealousy mostly. When you're a rich, hospitable man living in a house with a bunch of young, poor women, that's going to happen. On one occasion, she tried to slash my throat with a straight razor. I'd never had one of those against my throat before. And she did this because she said that I had flirted with a Spanish lady at the food court in Orange Walk Town. I didn't even remember seeing a Spanish lady at the food court worth looking at, but whatever.

Anyway, she had this blade against my throat, and I could feel the blood starting to run down my neck. In that moment, I thought, *This is a fucking serious situation*. I could feel the incredible slicing power of that straight blade, and I couldn't move away in either direction without getting cut wide open. I genuinely thought that she was going to kill me right there and then.

ME: What did you do?

John McAfee: I leaned back against the wall, put my hands up in the air, and calmly said, "Do it, Amy." Just like that. And she looked at me for a second and started laughing out loud, saying, "You…are special."

On another occasion, she tried to kill me with rat poison, but, knowing what rat poison smells like, I was wise to that. Then the next time, she tried to shoot me while I was sleeping and ended up blowing out my left eardrum. I'm still deaf in that ear today. For that, I made her go to her cabin on the property for a month without television. She screamed for days—"I didn't even shoot you. It's not fair without television." It was just a punishment, and I thought it was fair. She could have left and gone home if she didn't like it. I was never forcing anyone to stay with me.

However, it got to the point where I just couldn't trust her anymore. I certainly couldn't have her living with me when she was so unpredictable. I said to her, "Amy, you know I love you. But you are going to kill me one day."

ME: Did you kick her out?

John McAfee: Not quite. I agreed to build her a house in Carmelita instead and to pay for all her food and expenses thereafter. It sounds crazy when I say that now. But at the time, the idea made total sense because she loved it there, and her family was from there.

We went to Carmelita, found her a piece of property that she liked, and started building the house. Just before the thatched-roofed place was complete, there was a fatal shooting outside it in the street right outside her house.

I had no idea what was going on, but when I started inquiring, I found out that Carmelita specifically was the center for all of the drug activities in Orange Walk District. I started paying attention, and gradually I started piecing together who all the main drug dealers were and where the lots from which they sold drugs were located in the village. I didn't like that.

ME: What did you do about it?

John McAfee: I shut the whole operation down by force. I didn't specifically hurt anyone. But when I say force, I'll tell you what I mean. I went to my friend Eddie Ancona and said, "Eddie, we've got a problem. There's a huge drug problem in Carmelita. Amy's going to be living there. There are shootings outside her house, and I can't tolerate that." He said, "OK, I'm going to introduce you to somebody," and the person he introduced me to was the guy I mentioned earlier, Rodwell Richards, the most feared hit man in Central America.

ME: Describe this man for me.

John McAfee: Big, black, and very rough. My current wife Janice met him once when he came to San Francisco after I'd left Belize. He was an ex-police captain of such brutality that he was always on the precipice of being fired. His claim to fame had been that, when he was still with the police force, the previous prime minister, Said Musa, tasked him with shutting down the Los Zetas Cartel's activity in Belize. They'd been coming across the border from Mexico and doing whatever they wanted. Whenever they were arrested, someone would pay off the judges, and the judges would let them off. Rodwell Richards single-handedly put a stop to the Los Zetas infiltration.

Within six months of him being hired to do the job, every Zeta who entered Belize was either found dead in Belize somewhere or was shot while trying to escape. After he left the police, he started up on his own with this band of thirty or so vicious thugs, doing exclusively private contracts and whacking people. He was a heavy dude. Everybody in Central America knew the name Rodwell Richards.

And now, sometime in 2010, here he was, standing in front of me. I told him what the problem was and said, "What can I do about these drug dealers?" to which he replied, "Well, I can remove them all." "What does that mean?" I asked. "It means…remove," he said. "Oh no, you misunderstand. That's not what I want. Can't you just threaten them or something?"

Rodwell stared at me with the coldest imaginable eyes I'll never forget and said, "I don't threaten. I *do*."

Holy shit. I knew I was now in dangerous territory. But I also knew that he was in business to make money. So I told him that I was offering him a lot of money to do whatever it took to scare these drug dealers away. "I'll think about it," he said. The next day, he called me back and said, "I'll do it," shortly followed by the words, "Stay out of Carmelita," which I did.

ME: Having paid him, what did you think he was going to do?

JOHN MCAFEE: I didn't see what he did with my own eyes, but I heard enough from other people to understand what went down. Rodwell Richards knew exactly where every goddamn drug dealer in Carmelita lived. So in a convoy of cars with his helpers, he showed up at each house with body bags. He put a body bag on the ground outside each house, knocked on the door, and said, "This body bag has your name on it. I'm going to come back at noon. If you're still here, you're going to be in this bag just after noon." And sure enough, by noon, every drug dealer in Carmelita and the surrounding area was fucking gone. They knew that Rodwell Richards didn't bluff anyone. They have not come back to this day.

ME: You had to feel good about how it had all happened. Yes?

JOHN MCAFEE: Initially, I thought I've just cleaned up Carmelita and that that was a was a very good thing. And then, I realized that it really wasn't such a good thing because the assistant prime minister, Gaspar Vega, in his capacity as the head of drug dealing in the whole fucking district, was the guy who stood to lose most from what I'd just done.

While the minister of national defense at the time was doing various deals with the cartels that allowed them to travel freely across the border with Mexico, Gaspar Vega was selling drugs—drugs that he probably acquired from the minister of national defense—directly to the people of Orange Walk. Overnight, I had killed 50 percent of his business. That, my friend, was the final, final straw for me in Belize.

ME: Where did the antibiotics research you got into in Belize fit into all of this?

John McAfee: This was happening around the same time, and it all combined to bring about a set of terrible circumstances. The venture started after I went down to the southern resorts to look at a smaller private island that someone told me was for sale and I might like.

The southern resorts were nowhere near as nice as the San Pedro resorts in the north. In the north, the reef was close to the beach, and the waters on the beach were always dead calm regardless of what nightmares were happening out beyond the reef. In the south, that reef was miles offshore. Consequently, the waters in the south were always rougher, with big waves continually pounding the shore.

So we get to this private island—me, Amy, and a couple of the other girls—and as nice as it was, it looked like it was ready to get washed away at any second by the waves that were continually washing up all around, almost right up to the structures themselves.

While we were there, there was a girl there in a restaurant playing guitar and singing love songs. Her name was Allison Adonizio, and as it turned out, she was a PhD student from some university in Florida, and her area of specialty was something called quorum sensing. She was taking a break from her studies and was considering using Belize as a location to source rare plants for her studies.

ME: Briefly, what is quorum sensing?

John McAfee: Scientists discovered a dozen or so years ago that bacteria actually communicate, and they do so chemically. Whenever bacteria get into a specific environment, it produces a chemical for that specific environment: the acidic environment in the stomach or just under the skin or inside your nose, etc. As they start to replicate, they produce substances almost like pheromones. At the same time, they have receptors that detect other pheromones. The quorum is reached when there are enough bacteria to form what's called a biomass, a level at which bacteria can do actual damage to the body. However, some plants are capable of silencing that quorum, in effect deafening bacteria to the presence of these other pheromones. The bacteria, therefore, never become pathogenic, and the body can remove them without being handicapped.

ME: So you employed her right there and then?

John McAfee: Pretty much. I agreed that she'd come to my compound, where I would set her up with all the necessary research equipment in one of the buildings that was basically sitting empty. I then bought centrifuges, microscopes, and sensing gear. You name it, I got it. She came to live at the compound to do her research, and I agreed to pay her a trivial salary.

ME: Did you actually achieve anything with this research?

John McAfee: Yes, we did. We found a couple of plants, both of them very strange and hard to find, that achieved this quorum-sensing effect. We were really onto something, to the extent that we had enough to create 15,000 vials of a topical spray that could be applied to the skin. Sadly, most people in jungle environments died because of what seem like trivial infections. But this concoction of ours worked so well on the cases that we trialed that people from the villages were literally trying to break our door down to get their hands on it. I truly believed that this was going to be one of the greatest breakthroughs since the invention of penicillin.

ME: So why didn't that happen?

John McAfee: Well, the prime minister, at Mr. Vega's request, I assume, sent his gang suppression unit, led by Marco Vidal, to my house and raided the place—not that I was even a gang—claiming that they'd been tipped off that we were actually manufacturing methamphetamine, not antibiotics/antiseptics. They knew we weren't doing that; they found no such thing in the search. They just wanted an excuse to control me, and once they'd trashed the compound and removed all our records, etc., they threw me in jail on a bogus firearms charge because they said that I didn't have a license for one of the many guns I had on the property at the time.

ME: Did this raid come totally out of the blue?

John McAfee: Ever since I'd cleaned up Carmelita, I suspected it might go this way. Feeling threatened by what the government might try to do, I had been gradually beefing up my security. The house had become an armed fortress of sorts—but I was only defending myself, my staff, and my property from what I knew was an imminent threat.

To be fair, a week before the raid, a sort of peace offering was made. A senior figure in the UDP, one of Belize's two main political parties, came around. There was an election just around the corner. "Mr. McAfee," he said, "I know we've had some problems, and we'd like to resolve them. We thought that if you would simply donate $2 million to our campaign, this could all be cleared up." "You know what? I don't think so," I replied. That was a mistake.

The day after the raid, after I'd been released from jail with no charge, that same gentleman came back to see me and said, "We are so sorry. We were acting on a tip that was totally false. Can you forgive us? And, by the way, Mr. McAfee, have you now reconsidered that donation?"

Stupidly, I declined the offer again. And I did so because I'd been abused, been thrown in jail, had one of my dogs shot, and had had half a million dollars of my property destroyed. I was tired, confused, and raging at everyone at this point. "Get the fuck off my property," I said, which was a very stupid thing to say under the circumstances.

I then left Orange Walk forever, knowing I could never return to the jungle. Additionally, I did something that nobody in Belize would have expected: I took my army of security guards, most of whom were wild-eyed ex-cons, back to San Pedro with me, along with a growing troupe of young local girls.

ME: What was the significance of the guy from *Wired*, Joshua Davis, visiting you in 2012?

John McAfee: That whole thing was of no importance to me at all. I told you. He was naïve. I completely messed with him with a gun that he thought was loaded. And by doing so, I was making a point: we can have a perception of something, but if a single piece of information is missed or ignored, that perception then becomes very different from reality. So, the only person Josh Davis's interview was important to was Josh Davis, because he later wrote that book about me based just on a two-week period—a two-week period that meant nothing in the overall scheme of things.

ME: What happened to Allison Adonizio, who later accused you of rape in Nanette Burstein and Jeff Wise's movie *Gringo: The Dangerous Life of John McAfee*?

John McAfee: That's a complicated story. But let me explain. At the time when the jungle lab was making what I thought were exciting discoveries, I was simultaneously promoting the lab's work by having stories run by various science magazines back in the US. Jeff Wise, a journalist who'd done a story on me a few years earlier when I was pursuing the sport flying venture, came down to Belize in 2012 to write a story about the work we were doing with quorum sensing. Meanwhile, Allison turned out to be absolutely stark raving fucking crazy—at least as far as I could see.

Nevertheless, when she worked, which was not that frequently because she spent most of her time partying with the local boys in the jungle, she did a good job. Anyway, Jeff Wise came down in the middle of all this. He's a good-looking guy, and on the first night, it seemed to me that he and Allison got on very well, and that close friendship continued for the week he was there. Jeff then went back, wrote an OK story, and then Allison and I reached a point where we couldn't work together anymore. On my side, there was no animosity whatsoever. I'd have probably carried on by myself or found something else interesting to do.

However, she demanded half of the assets. I told her she was deluded. I'd paid for all the equipment, and the lab was on my property. She left in a rage and went back to the US. And at some point, she must have got together with Jeff Wise again, and between them, they must have decided that they just had to make a "let's rip this guy apart" type of movie. That's all that matters about the story, but her accusations about me are absurd.

I had a sense that Jeff Wise might have been in discussion with the Belizean authorities—specifically Marco Vidal, the leader of the gang suppression unit. Because they had little access to high-level press in the US, my suspicion was that the Belizean authorities had tipped Jeff off by saying, "There's a scoop coming."

Two days later, my compound was raided, and I was thrown in jail. But after some life-saving legal help from my ex-business manager Maria, who I mentioned before, I was released with no charge, all of which completely threw a spanner in the works of what I saw as being Jeff Wise's and the Belizean authorities' little plan. The day after I was released, Jeff Wise didn't even call me. He just flew home and continued writing bizarre stories about me from the safety of the US. Meanwhile, after getting let go with no charge, I then returned to San Pedro. That was the beginning of the end of real war with Belize.

ME: Did you have any direct contact with Nanette Burstein?

John McAfee: I'm not sure at what point Jeff and Allison connected with Nanette. All I knew was that they were shopping this idea for a movie around. When they found Nanette, given that all I personally see her as is a shit-stirrer who likes nothing more than to distort fiction into her version of fact, she was always going to be perfect for a movie like the one they had in mind.

However, I didn't actually know there was even going to be a movie until I was on my presidential campaign trail in 2016 and people said, "Did you know that Showtime is in town filming something about you?" I wasn't concerned and refused to be interviewed on camera by her. I have, however, had many spirited email exchanges with Nanette, in which I've given her none of the information that she wanted. That's all there is to say about that movie and the people involved in it.

ME: Was there any part of you that thought that was the time you should have just left Belize?

JOHN MCAFEE: No, not one single part of me. Belize was my fucking home. I'd invested a lot of time and energy into my life there. I had ongoing love affairs and legal residency. I failed to see why I should have been intimidated—especially by politicians. I had every right to take security and weapons back to San Pedro. I was in a country where everybody hated me. I had a right to defend myself.

But, overnight, this tourist beach village, where the locals sucked the tourists they hated so much dry of money, changed radically. It went from this idyllic place of calm ocean and sandy beaches to a place where you walked down the shore past a house that was fortified by black-shirted armed guards on every corner of the property and large, snarling guard dogs straining at leashes. People didn't like it; I didn't give a shit. I was determined to do things differently. "You just can't have people with guns on the beach," people who owned nearby businesses said. "Show me the law that says I can't," was my reply. These people had no idea what I'd experienced in the jungle. I wasn't going to let it happen again. I was digging on for the fight.

ME: I've read that there were many girls with you in this beach house.

JOHN MCAFEE: That is true. There were eight of them by this point, one of which, Samantha, is an important part of the story going forward. Each of them had their own separate bedrooms on the property; each of them took turns cooking. The press made out that this was an idyllic, hedonistic existence I was living in San Pedro at this point, but the reality was anything but idyllic. It was tense; I was in a permanent state of high alert and continually on the lookout for threats or a hint of betrayal from the various people who I was employing, none of whom I felt I could truly trust.

As it turned out, I had every reason to feel that way. At least two of the girls were being pressurized by local gang members to extort me or frame me. My staff had to be completely swapped out on more than one occasion because I suspected them of colluding with the authorities. Meanwhile, I slept in my bed in that house literally with one eye open and with a loaded shotgun pointed at the bedroom door while the coastguard ship cruised up and down the coast all night long, pausing only to shine the spotlight directly at the windows of my house.

ME: Which gangs were involved in threatening you?

John McAfee: I didn't know this at the time, but I found out later that Samantha had been taking money from all sorts of gangs. I also found out that it was she who had tipped off the police for the raid on my property in the jungle. She'd been living in the jungle compound at the time; she was even working in the lab. She was the inside girl and was paid a certain amount of money to turn. When she saw the shit that went down, when I went back to San Pedro, I think she felt some remorse for a while. But when she saw the women count going up, she got pissed again and contacted these two gangs to ask if they could help her get my money or whatever.

She was acting on jealousy, with retrospect. But at some point, I was sent a written note telling me to deposit a large sum of money under a bridge between the north and south island or else people would come to San Pedro and kill me and all my guards. I had no idea who sent this note. At the time, I thought it could have been a government setup, or stupid kids, or one of two gangs I knew Samantha had links with. Whoever sent the note, I knew it was a serious threat.

The White Lobster Gang was one such gang. White Lobster was the name given to packages of cocaine that washed in on Belize's beaches. Passing cartel boats from Colombia that were going up and down the coast either dumped this stuff in high-speed chases or their boats broke up in bad weather. Either way, tons of cocaine washed up on Belize's beaches, and this gang was ruthless towards anyone that tried to steal it. A few tried and got caught. Their mutilated bodies were left on the beach as a warning to anyone else that might consider it.

The other possibility was the George Street Gang, Belize's most notorious organized crime gang. There were connections to this crew within my security group and, indeed, connections to the highest levels of the Belizean government via the gang members. Either in combination or separately, they tried to trap me on a couple of occasions, in one instance by sending a girl, also called Amy, to my house as bait. And on another by sending art, which they also knew I liked.

ME: This really is like a movie. What did you think was going to happen?

John McAfee: I wasn't sure what was going to go down. But whatever it was, I knew that it wasn't going to end in some movie-style gunfight on the beach in San Pedro, that much was for sure. We were all heavily armed. To engage in that kind of fiasco would have drawn far too much attention, and, furthermore, they knew that all the people who were working for me were crazed ex-cons anyway. These guys had been in jail, some of them several times. They'd have fought because they had nothing to lose. There was no way they were going back to jail.

Instead, I feared something more insidious and subtle might be being planned, some complicated set of circumstances that would allow them to frame me with something and then quietly bring me in. I must warn you, though: we are reaching a part of this story where I must be careful.

ME: Why is that?

John McAfee: Most of the people I'm going to talk about are still alive and still living in Belize. Not only that but some of them are still known to be my friends. So I'm not going to be as forthright about certain things as I have been with you, my friend, and I just want you to understand why that is.

ME: It feels like it isn't a coincidence that, as we approach the part of the story where your next-door neighbor gets killed, you are now telling me you can't be forthright. What would you think if you were in my position?

John McAfee: I am not going to lie to you. I never have. But by saying too much about something, I could be putting people at risk. When I left Belize, everyone I'd been associated with got pulled in by the police, including my good friend Eddie Ancona, who spent six weeks in Hattieville, one of the worst prisons on Earth. They killed my boat captain; various other people that I'm about to talk about got seriously harassed or jailed, or, in some cases, both

So if I do much more by way of outing people, I could do serious damage. That's all I'm saying. If it was just me that was at risk, that would be fine. I'm on the run anyway, so I don't give a shit. But it's not just me, and I accept that none of this material is standard material for a book like this: hit men, corrupt government officials, prostitutes, and violent gang culture. But believe me, this really was the world I found myself in during those last months in that country. The wrong word from me really could get people killed in a place like Belize. That said, anything I do say to you, you may write.

ME: Speaking of getting killed, what was the background between you and Gregory Faull?

John McAfee: People said that my neighbor Gregory Faull and I were enemies, but the reality was that I hadn't spoken more than fifty words to the man in five years. He had retired down there, his father visited from time to time, and he was just nice and, frankly, unremarkable. When I brought my dogs back from the jungle, I won't lie: they did bark a lot. I admit they made a lot of noise. He complained, but so did everyone else in the fifteen or so houses that were nearby on the shore. He certainly did not stand out in any way, shape, or form as someone who was aggrieved more than anyone else.

However, my dogs were poisoned one Friday night. The British Royal Marine I'd employed as my head of security because I was tired of dealing with lying Belizeans woke me early in the morning and told me that something had happened outside. I grabbed my gun, went out, and all the dogs were lying, whimpering in agony, with their guts spewing out of their mouths and asses. I had to shoot them all in the head there and then. One of them was Amy's, the girl who'd tried to kill me several times. As I shot it, it was looking up at me with a face that said, "I am glad you are here." The guards took them and had them buried.

ME: When you found the dogs, what did you think was going on?

JOHN MCAFEE: Well, it further confirmed what I'd been feeling in the weeks since I'd returned from the jungle: that something serious was afoot. This was the beginning of the assault. They were creating a situation whereby the police could just walk in with an arrest warrant and collect me in broad daylight. If that had happened, such is the corruption within that country, I'd either still be there now, or I'd be lying dead in a ditch somewhere.

But I had no clue who had poisoned my dogs. Gregory Faull certainly wouldn't have. He had dogs of his own. What man who had dogs would poison someone else's? And then, twenty-four hours later, when Gregory Faull was found dead, I knew what was coming down. I *knew*....

ME: I have to ask: Did you have anything to do with his death?

JOHN MCAFEE: I am many things, but stupid isn't one of them. How stupid would I have had to have been to do such a thing given my circumstances? Please, God.

ME: Do you know who did?

JOHN MCAFEE: I always had my suspicions. But that's all I'm prepared to say.

ME: What happened next? Why did you ultimately flee?

John McAfee: By this point, I knew beyond doubt I was being framed. I also knew I'd get no justice in a country like Belize if I was captured. I couldn't just run initially, because that's what they expected me to do. At that point, I had no means of getting off the island by boat, road, or air. So I did what anyone would do: I sat tight at home and waited for the next move.

And I didn't have to wait for long. At nine o'clock the next morning, a boat containing fifteen members of the Belize police force docked not outside my house, but further down the beach. From there, I saw them walking in single file and with purpose up the beach towards my house. Instead of panicking, I calmly walked into my master bedroom, walked into my safe room, closed two doors—one of them solid steel—behind me, and climbed into an invisible attic recess above the closet via a pull-down ladder. There, I lay silently on a piece of plywood for eighteen hours while the police turned my house upside down.

ME: Were you afraid at this point?

John McAfee: No, I was in self-preservation mode. I knew what had to be done. I just had to wait, while I could hear the police walking around in the house below me. It wasn't comfortable. Next time I do this, I must remember to leave a mattress and some water. By that evening, I could hear no sound, either on the property or outside. So I silently came down from the attic, slipped out the back door of my bedroom, sneaked as quietly as I could to my other neighbor's house, and let myself in through a side door. While they weren't in the country, they left a key with me to look after their property, which I did out of kindness. From here, I called Samantha and told her to put a plan in place in conjunction with a taxi driver. We had to get to Belize City. As I said, we couldn't risk running. Instead, we'd be hiding in plain sight.

TEN

ESCAPE

The very few people who knew that I was talking to McAfee have asked me the same question: "Do you think he killed that guy down in Belize?" I never answered, of course, but I gave it plenty of thought.

I went into our conversations wanting to believe that he didn't. Indeed, I knew that if he did, no matter how interesting any book was, it would always have the shadow of an innocent man's murder hanging over it.

So, honestly, I was prepared for the worst-case scenario. And that scenario was one where we talked about the events surrounding Gregory Faull's death on November 21, 2012, and afterward, I didn't believe a single word McAfee said. Had that been the case, I would have finished our talks, pressed "save" on the Word document of transcriptions, and walked away. I promised I would have. No book is worth the negativity that an attachment to violent murder brings.

But I didn't feel like that when McAfee explained the events to me. And having worked with many people from all walks of life, some of them extremely narcissistic and unpredictable, I like to think I know when people are telling me the truth.

Despite the allegations made in *Gringo: The Dangerous Life of John McAfee*, at no point did I ever feel that McAfee was involved in Gregory Faull's death. He may well have done many suspect things in Belize. I always felt uncomfortable with the concept of him keeping the company of many girls at once, for example. Regardless of what I already knew about his complex relationships with women, I could never quite get my head around the idea of him having what was essentially a harem.

I also knew that he had started taking a variety of drugs again in Belize. But in that instance, his reasons for having done so perfectly tied in with justifications he explained previously regarding only reaching for drugs out of absolute necessity. In Belize, under siege and suspicious of everyone and everything, few could argue that that necessity was certainly there.

But having heard him tell me his life story in detail up until 2012, I genuinely felt that these few years in Belize were merely an extension of the life the man had always lived. Not just that, he had lived it unapologetically and without any obvious sense of guilt. The difference was that in Belize, a place where due process and common law seemingly went out the window at every turn, the stakes were very much higher. That environment simply accentuated the McAfee tendency for being wary. And it reached a point where it seemed he had every reason to be.

ME: What was the plan once you got to Belize City? Surely you were taking a huge risk by being, essentially, in plain sight.

John McAfee: Sam and I had arranged to hide out in the upstairs attic of a Chinese warehouse in downtown Belize City, really not far at all from the main police station on Queen Street. It was a pleasant room, very well equipped and air-conditioned, and I knew that nobody would ever find us there because the Chinese owners, well versed in the art of secrecy as they were, weren't going to say shit to anybody. As safe houses go, it was one of the better ones. And it's here that I was active on my blog, every second of every day. All this time, I was hatching an escape plan, and while I was, my photo was fucking everywhere. This exposure would soon play to my advantage because, in parallel with working the blog to keep this story alive and breathing, I was teaching Sam the finer nuances of disguise.

ME: Did you both wear disguises? Were they credible?

John McAfee: Even basic techniques like going to the bathroom and stuffing rolled-up toilet paper in your cheeks. It sounds mundane, but I promise you that when you walk out, even your own mother wouldn't recognize you. These are the things you have to do when you're in a pinch, and I knew we'd need every edge we could get in the days ahead.

As the primary person of interest to the police, I required a more radical makeover. And I quickly figured that the first thing I'd be expected to do after going on the run was to shave off my distinctive goatee beard. Everybody would have shaved it off. *No. The beard stays,* I thought.

Instead, I manicured it precisely and made it jet-black. Then I dyed my hair the same color, like those old men in their eighties you sometimes see, who are trying to look twenty. I got a cane and started practicing how to walk with it and a hunched back. Before long, I had a brand-new persona, a tragic excuse for an old, vain man it admittedly was. But, crucially, nobody in his or her right mind was ever going to look at me and say, "That's John McAfee."

Again, it worked. Belize City is a bustling, vibrant, colorful place at the best of times, and it got to the point where I could go out with Sam to the grocery store unnoticed. We had to—because the Chinese barely acknowledged our existence, far less fed us. To the casual observer, I was just this old man with a black goatee and matching, lustrous hair, walking around grocery shopping with his granddaughter holding his arm to help him along.

ME: Are you saying that nobody looked at you twice?

John McAfee: Nobody paid any fucking attention, even though we were in such close proximity to the police station and in plain sight, as you say. Meanwhile, I knew that the police effort was not letting up. They were still diligently hunting us, and they'd never stop. This went on for three weeks while I plotted my escape.

It soon became obvious to me that if I were going to get out of the country alive, I'd need outside help. There I was, one white older guy with Samantha, a young Spanish girl. Together, it was going to be hard to get across any border. And I wasn't prepared for us to separate and to let her go it alone because there was always the possibility that she'd be caught and tortured for information about my whereabouts. That would have been unthinkable. I figured that as long as Samantha and I were together, there would be no reason to harm her.

But I needed assistance, preferably in the guise of white people. So I told Amy, who, despite having a mother who was as black as the night sky, could pass as a white woman, to co-opt her white boyfriend, Keith. I knew he'd do anything she told him to. But that still gave us just three white people and Sam—not exactly enough to fill a tourist bus that could be driven around Belize unnoticed. We had to be a bigger group that would look more authentic and draw less attention.

ME: Some would argue that a bigger group might attract more attention?

John McAfee: I didn't think so. I started thinking about possibilities. My first thought was the media. Ever since the early days of McAfee Associates, I'd always known how to, depending on how you viewed it, work or work with the press.

Furthermore, I knew, given these extreme circumstances, that I'd be getting offers from people all over the world wanting to either interview me and/or physically travel with me during my escape. I was in no doubt as to how big a scoop my situation would be for any publication.

ME: Surely there's a conflict here? On one hand, you want not to be seen, but on the other, you want publicity? Explain....

John McAfee: The first person I chose was a gentleman by the name of Adam Thomson, who worked for the *Financial Times* in London. "Send me a current photograph of yourself," I told him during our initial dialogue. When it arrived, well damn me if he didn't just look like this typical, English, distinguished gentleman. I thought to myself, *I can pull this shit off....*

Given careful planning, the group dynamics could add up. Sam would be part of this guy's paid entourage for female companionship. I would be his Central American advisor (a role that is almost always performed out by a white guy, incidentally). Amy and Keith would be his grandchildren. We'd all appear to be down there in Belize having fun.

ME: And this journalist bought into all of this?

John McAfee: In exchange for an exclusive story? Absolutely. He came. When he arrived, he was blindfolded, driven around Belize City, dropped off at a random bus station, was told "follow me" by a passing stranger before being delivered to a street corner, whereupon I showed up alone and hobbled close by, this old man, whispering, again, "Follow me, sir." I then led him up to the attic.

"I can't do this," he said, within literally a few minutes.

"What is it that you can't do, sir?" I asked him.

"I just can't go with you," he began, scanning the room wide-eyed at the bizarre posse in his midst. "I didn't understand the gravity of what I was getting into."

Hearing this, Sam jumped up. She was pissed.

"I'm twenty-one, I'm a girl, and I have bigger balls than you do. Put that in your article."

He almost did. I doubt that the piece Adam Thomson wrote on his return from Belize was what he had in mind when he went down there, but it was certainly reflective of his disquiet about the air of chaos, and rightly so. Yes, we were acting out roles, me in disguise, but it wasn't any sort of game we were playing. We were fleeing for our lives from a ruthless pursuant in a country where justice was hard to come by.

On reflection, I can't exactly blame the guy for getting freaked out and bailing. *The Financial Times of London* isn't exactly renowned for being the most overly adventurous crowd. Nevertheless, I received a bunch of other offers over the following few days. But as much as I knew how valuable coverage would be, I resisted these advances. Instead, I trusted my intuition. I could sense beyond doubt that these, too, were people who would either freak out, panic, or just do something that would get us caught, simply because they didn't have the necessary experience.

ME: Were lots of publications/outlets really contacting you? It was suggested that you were exaggerating this fact to spin your own story.

John McAfee: Many of them, via my blog, which by this time was getting a lot of attention in the press. Then along came *VICE* magazine in the form of an email from editor-in-chief Rocco Castoro. He said that he wanted to come down to Belize with world-renowned war photographer Robert King, who, despite seeming to be somewhat crazy in the head, had been around the block. Looking into him more while I deliberated for a few hours, I found that he'd been on the frontline several times in a few wars and been shot in the ass for his troubles. *Goddamn, does he have balls!* I thought.

We agreed that they'd come down. I'd get two more bodies to aid my escape; they'd get a story. That was the deal, and it seemed like a fair trade. In advance, I had tasked a cab driver I knew well, one of the only people whom I still believed was not being paid by the Belizean government, I might add, to rent a van with "Turismo" on the side. He then came and picked Sam and me up first. As he did so, I was acutely aware that we were switching modes of living. We'd been in hiding, but movement changed that status. Now we were on the run.

After collecting Amy and Keith, the *VICE* guys were then met at the Belize City airport, and the six of us then headed south on the Coastal Highway, running the police gauntlet as we did. However, I had everything planned to the finest detail, even down to weather reports.

I knew that there would be roadblocks on every road in Belize, manned by police officers looking for me, possibly holding my photograph. I also knew that, especially in third-world countries, policemen who are paid five dollars per day do not stand in the pouring rain checking IDs. No, they vacate to their automobiles. Who wouldn't? They'd sit huddled in these vehicles, and, of course, they might look at a passing van and think, *I suppose that dude might have looked somewhat like the guy in the photograph.* But I was counting on them not actually venturing out and getting soaked to find out for sure.

And that's how this ruse all played out. Just a few minutes after we met Rocco and Robert, there was, as per my calculations, a deluge that would ultimately last until the following day. We cruised past roadblock after checkpoint, occasionally maneuvering from one side of the van to the other to make it appear more populated than it was. I even have photographs taken out of the van window of police in their dark green Jeeps, looking at us as we passed, with my photograph pinned to the dashboard. Yet, they seemingly saw no reason whatsoever to stop us.

ME: I'm struggling to understand how you planned to get out of the country? Surely you'd have to cross a border somewhere?

John McAfee: Our initial destination was the small, coastal town of Dangriga, a little over eighty miles away and the place where I'd arranged a fishing boat to be waiting. I knew the place well. I'd visited often under more relaxed circumstances to go fishing around the reef or to explore the many Mayan ruins in the surrounding jungle.

I'd checked us in for a night in a hotel that I'd frequented on several occasions prior. It was this gorgeous plantation-style retreat at the top of a mountain overlooking the ocean. Under normal circumstances, the hotel staff would have known me. But in my disguise, they didn't recognize me at all, which was both helpful and necessary given my fugitive status. It was only the next morning as we were leaving that I let the façade slip somewhat. I started standing up straight, looking at them, smiling, and speaking in a normal voice. "Mr. McAfee, is that you?" the desk clerk whispered through narrowed, quizzical eyes. "Indeed," I nodded sheepishly. "I sincerely apologize."

What else could I say? I can't deny that I hated pulling a trick on people who'd previously been kind and friendly. Nevertheless, you do what you've got to do. I just couldn't run the risk of anyone turning me in. Desperate measures force similarly desperate acts, my friend.

ME: Was this the point where you said goodbye to the girls?

John McAfee: Yes, and it was all a bit strange and unexpectedly emotional for me. We gathered at the boat that awaited us. Everything was on time and going precisely to plan. It was the moment for long embraces and painful goodbyes. And at this point, things became far more emotionally complicated for me than I ever bargained for.

Amy and I had talked in the past about her coming with Sam and me and leaving her boyfriend Keith in Belize. I knew I'd never be able to come back, and because of that, if she stayed, I knew that I'd never, ever get her out. For her to come was the only chance that we had of staying in each other's lives.

However, as I stood beside the boat facing Sam and Amy, these two young women for whom I had such deep affection, I saw a look cross their faces at the same time. It was the same expression, and it said, "We're at war, bitch." These young girls both knew that they were now running for their lives. And it was as if there was this simultaneous dawning that only one of them would be getting on board that fishing boat. The other would be remaining in Belize, albeit in Amy's case, I always knew she'd be safe because she'd be living with her white boyfriend Keith in San Pedro. Nobody would touch them there. Let me be clear: I would not have left her if there had been any risk of future danger.

Regardless, for me, it was still a hopeless situation, a dire dilemma of the heart. One thing that was for certain was that there was no way in hell I could take them both on the run. An older man with one young girl in tow was just about acceptable. Two young women, on the other hand, jealous and at each other's throats, would have alerted far more suspicion and would have put all of our lives in danger. I couldn't take that risk. I had to make a choice, and, in doing so, I have to admit to being motivated only by self-preservation.

ME: Let's forget that I do not for a second understand your attachment to these girls, given one tried to kill you several times and the other colluded with gangs to potentially have you killed or extorted, but how did you make a choice?

John McAfee: For some time, I'd known that Samantha's uncle was the former attorney general of Guatemala, Telesforo Guerra. Despite no longer holding that position, he still wielded considerable power in a country whose relationship with neighboring Belize wasn't exactly warm and fuzzy. Indeed, they'd been haggling over a worthless, barely populated slice of jungle on their shared border for a hundred years or so. I knew, therefore, that once I was out of Belize, away from the fucked-up jurisdiction of Prime Minister Dean Barrow, with his paid-off gangs and personal armies, that he wouldn't be able to touch me easily. He certainly wasn't in a position to be able to just call up and say, "Hey, Pres. Dean Barrow here. Would you mind apprehending that fucker McAfee who has just walked into your kingdom?'" I knew that was not going to happen. At the very least, he'd need to go through standard diplomatic channels with the powers that be in Guatemala—and even then, I'm sure that they had way bigger fish to fry diplomatically than me.

So, due to her personal connections with a once-powerful dude who I knew might be extremely helpful to us down the line in Guatemala, I chose Samantha over Amy, and I did not enjoy doing so. I just couldn't save them both. As I broke the news at the boat, I'll never forget the expression on Amy's face. It said just one word: *Why?* I think she felt I'd been giving her false hope along which, truthfully, I had been. It was a terrible moment. Her face still haunts me now. You are in a very sensitive period of my life now, my friend.

This was one of the strangest moments of all of my many hours with John McAfee. As he described leaving Belize, and how he arrived at the decision to leave one of the girls behind, he sobbed uncontrollably. I've listened to the recording hundreds of times since, and the seven minutes and thirty-nine seconds of listening to the man crying uncontrollably are no easier to listen to now than they were in March of 2020.

Part of me had no idea what to say. So I said nothing. Another bigger part of me didn't really understand what it was that was upsetting him so much. After all, the way I saw it, there were several other events in his long life: the death of his father, lack of relationship with his kids, and lost love, etc., that arguably warranted a similar if not more emotional outburst. I couldn't understand it then, and I still can't now.

But these emotions he was showing were in no way put-on for dramatic effect. These were real. This was a man who really did feel the painful loss of a Belizean girl who had tried to kill him three times, deeply. To me, few things exemplified the absolute mystery of the man I'd been talking to for months more than those seven or so minutes. They will forever puzzle me, as he also will. After a ten-minute break, we continued.

John McAfee: We set off. Destination: Livingston, Guatemala. As the coast came into closer view, I started considering an imminent hurdle that I'd always known we'd have to negotiate. Because we'd left Belize illegally, we'd be arriving at the Guatemalan border without a passport exit stamp. That's a big no-no anywhere, especially in Central America. However, I'd already planned the solution in advance.

In all Latin American countries, eating and meals are viewed as sacred things. Maybe this view is rooted in a history of deprivation and the lack of sufficient food, or perhaps there's some deeper religious reason. Either way, all I knew was that you just don't fuck with people's meals. We arrived in Livingston, Guatemala's only port on the Caribbean side, and I had planned it specifically so that we would arrive as close to 1 p.m. as possible.

ME: What possible difference did that make?

John McAfee: There were two reasons for this. Firstly, I knew that the siesta, the most sacred and beloved of Spanish inventions, did not apply to government employees. Beyond that, I knew that we'd be arriving in a deserted ghost town. Restaurants…closed. Stores…shutters down.

Secondly, I also felt sure that whoever was on duty would likely be the lowest on the totem pole and also the most unhappy about having to nap in the back of the immigration office on some tiny cot, only then to be disturbed by a bunch of fucking Americans. When we landed, I was beyond apologetic.

"Sir," I began, with hands in a subservient prayer position, "we haven't eaten in many hours because we've been at sea. Please could you grant us the freedom to go to the restaurant up the hill, grab a bite to eat, and come back after the siesta?"

"Of course!" he said, clearly respectful, as I knew he would be, of how important food is to any human. Meanwhile, I also knew very well that he didn't want to process us anyway. All he wanted to do was go back, lie down, and hope nobody else arrived for the next two or three hours.

We walked to the restaurant, ordered, ate, stood up, walked down the hill to the dock, and climbed aboard the other boat I'd arranged to pick us up, a hollowed-out canoe with an outboard engine on the back, essentially, to take us all the way up the Rio Dulce to the town of Fronteras. We never went back to the immigration office.

ME: What was the specific appeal of Fronteras? Did you know people there?

John McAfee: I'd heard about Fronteras from friends who were into sailing. "Sailing up the Rio Dulce is the most profound of all things," people said—and, holy shit, were they right. At the end of the river, you enter the vast expanse of Lake Izabal and see the distant lights of the small town of Fronteras at the end, winking like a beacon. Boat is the only way to get there except for the very roughest of back roads.

Perhaps for this reason, Fronteras is probably the safest place on the planet. And given our predicament, it needed to be. Did I know people there? Good God, no. In fact, the town was filled with nothing but people who were evading the law. Fraud, assassinating a prime minister—whatever it was, it seemed like they were all in Fronteras, Guatemala. People had no last names. It was considered rude to even ask anyone's last name. Police were nonexistent. As soon as we arrived in Fronteras, I knew we were going to be fine there. For the time being, we were out of immediate danger, I thought.

ME: I remember reading this story at the time. It was all over the news. Is this where you had your cover blown?

John McAfee: Yes, and what a fucking shitshow it was. And we would have been except, having got us booked into a hotel for what I figured might need to be a couple of months in hiding, we went down to the swimming pool, whereupon Rocco, in his capacity as the senior editor of *VICE* magazine, showed his complete lack of experience.

"I want a picture of John and me at the pool here," he suddenly said. "We're going to publish it on our website right now." "Cool," I said, "but make sure you scrub the location data." "Yes, yes, of course," he replied, without looking up from what he was doing. But he was in such a rush, so desperate for the scoop after days of being sworn to silence as part of our deal until we reached the relative safety of Guatemala, that he obviously lost his fucking mind. The picture was indeed published on the front page of *VICE*'s website with the accompanying caption: *We Are with John McAfee Right Now, Suckers.*

I kid you not: within thirty seconds of that image going online, the telephones started ringing in the hotel. The reason? Every motherfucker on the internet now knew exactly where we were. The location data was still on there. There were Google Earth images with a large X where we were standing not thirty seconds prior.

ME: Why did he do this? It put you all at risk, surely.

John McAfee: I have no idea. As I said, as experienced as Robert King was, and I'm still in contact with him today, maybe Rocco was more interested in the attention the story would get than keeping everyone safe. I didn't hold it against him at the time. There was no point. Now things had changed though. Unwittingly, I'd just dumped some serious pressure on the government of Guatemala. Up until that point, everything was vague. I was just some schmuck who had escaped, and maybe I'd made it into Guatemala, or maybe nobody really knew where the fuck I'd gone.

Now though, if anyone so much as thought about googling the word Guatemala, it jumped out of the screen. It was near the very top of most-searched words. News sites all over the world were all over it: *Guatemala. McAfee. McAfee In Guatemala.* That shit was everywhere.

ME: In tangible terms, what did you think might happen?

John McAfee: Well, good God, I had experienced enough of Central American mentality to know that, in these circumstances, the Guatemalan government wasn't just going to shrug and say, "He's here, so what?" No, now that the world at large knew what was unfolding on their watch, I knew they'd be wary of potential embarrassment. The authorities were going to do anything they could to pick me up immediately. They weren't going to let me sit in Fronteras and fucking sunbathe.

So, having been on the run, and before I could even sit my tired ass down on the bed I was about to sleep on, I found myself on the run again, only this time not from some third-world hick prime minister. No, Guatemala had one of the most disciplined, well-trained, and vicious armies in all of Central America. Because of a careless error by a rookie magazine journalist, the stakes had gotten very much higher.

ME: Now that you'd been discovered, what was the game plan?

John McAfee: We had to leave again. We'd just gone from the frying pan into the fire. We had a different bunch of bastards after me. By the time a taxi arrived and we were ready to leave, everybody at the front desk of the hotel knew exactly who I was. Everybody was looking at us in absolute horror because the stories that were circulating about my character were pretty intense, to say the least. People were afraid. By this point, I'd called Samantha's uncle to introduce myself. I'd never met him before. "Hi, I'm John McAfee," I said. "Oh, I know who you are, Mr. McAfee," he replied. "I would like representation," I told him. "Absolutely, I'm at your service," he said. "What can I do for you?" "You can get me back to America," I told him. "No problem. That'll be $100,000."

ME: Did you have $100,000, and if so, how?

John McAfee: I have always had emergency money throughout my life that I'd never had cause to dip into. This money was safe for a situation where my world was about to come to an end. If anything qualified as that kind of an emergency, this was it. I made a call back to the US—I don't need to tell you to whom—got the man $100,000, whereupon he assured me he'd get me to America. The only problem I now had was getting to him, by running a gauntlet through Guatemalan police and soldiers who were sure to be on the lookout for me. The odds were not in my favor.

ME: Was part of you resigned to being collected at this point?

John McAfee: I had thought about it. If I was going to be collected, I wanted to be collected by Interpol and not by the Guatemalan authorities, that much I knew.

ME: What difference did it make? Collected is collected, isn't it?

John McAfee: If Interpol collected me, I'd have to go through all the standard Geneva Convention-type stuff where I'd have to be treated fairly. It wouldn't be great, but at least I'd be perfectly safe. If the Guatemalans had collected me, all bets were off. Who the fuck knows what horrors I would have had to endure? That was my biggest fear. To allay that fear, I had to get to Guatemala City, and let's just say that there was no Interpol in fucking Fronteras.

We arranged to meet Telesforo Guerra, who in turn had sent his men to meet us at a handover point somewhere between Guatemala City and Fronteras, on back roads. In the car were me, Samantha, and these two

VICE guys. But the problem I now had was that our cab driver soon figured out who we were.

ME: How?

John McAfee: I said to him, "Sir, do you have a telephone?" He handed me his phone. "Ah, a beautiful telephone it is," I said. "And I will give you $500 in cash for it right here and now." At that point, he figured it out. I gave him the cash, took the phone, broke it in half, and threw it into the jungle as we drove along the road. This was in a country where the average daily wage was five dollars.

ME: How did this poor cab driver respond to that?

John McAfee: He turned dark. And by dark, I mean he got fucking scared. He stopped joking and started looking very fearful and panicked. I'd just given him the equivalent of a year's wages. I'm sure he suspected that nothing good could come from such a start to our relationship; I could see those thoughts going through his head. Meanwhile, I was the only person in that car that spoke even a smidgeon of Spanish. However, I did not have enough Spanish to calm this motherfucker down.

ME: How did you appease this poor guy?

John McAfee: I tried another tactic, the kind of tactic that my programming friend Dennis Yelle from back in my McAfee days would not have understood. "Señor, what kind of music do you have?" I said, pointing to the stereo tape deck on his dashboard. "I have many," he replied. "What's your favorite?" I asked him. And so he pulled out a cassette tape. And by this time, this guy was quite cheery again, despite having a bunch of white men in his cab, one of whom was wanted for murder and had just snapped his phone and thrown it out of a moving car in exchange for a year's wages in cash, and a Spanish-looking chick that looked as if she might do anything at any time. The tape went in the machine, and on came "Gimme Shelter" by the Rolling Stones. As soon as he did that,

I thought, *Well, fuck, it's all going to be cool. We're all going to have fun here,* and immediately started singing along with the tape. Music was the only means of communication I had. Robert King, who was sitting in the front seat at the time, video recorded all of this. It's out there online somewhere if you care to look.

ME: I assume you made it to the safety of Guatemala City without incident?

JOHN MCAFEE: More or less. We got to the halfway point, where everybody was happy apart from Rocco Castoro, who, as it turned out, had sold me a bill of goods about his level of experience when I was vetting people to come down to help me escape just by being present. He told me he'd been in every war in the Middle East, etc., etc., but he sure as hell didn't act as if he had. He acted like some terrified geek who was ready to piss his pants. And I later found out from Robert King, who really is legitimate, that Rocco went to cover situations in the Middle East, but only after it was over. He had claimed that was *war* coverage, but really, it wasn't.

ME: Do you think he had exaggerated his experiences to convince you to get him on board?

JOHN MCAFEE: He certainly puffed up his credentials, and none of that was of help to us, especially when, as we ate lunch at a restaurant at the pick-up point while waiting to be met, he kept nervously looking out the door. Before I could say something, Robert said, "Rocco, if you do that one more time, I swear I'll kill you myself." Robert knew that we weren't safe until we got to Guatemala City. Robert knew we were in fucking no man's land with one of the most brutal paramilitary forces on Earth looking for us. Eventually, the car, Telesforo's big, black Mercedes limousine, showed up, and we were taken to Guatemala City.

ME: At this point, did you think the danger was over?

John McAfee: I knew that now that we were in his company, it didn't matter if the police had a goddamn roadblock down the road. I had made a deal. He had accepted my money. If that bastard wasn't able to help me, there was no hope for anything. To that end, I knew we would be safe, even if there were a thousand soldiers with AK-47s pointed at us, because Telesforo Guerra was one of the most feared men in Central America. So, while everyone around me was probably still panicking, I stopped worrying the moment I got into that limousine. I didn't want to be in this play any more than anyone else. But whether I liked it or not, I was in it. We got to Guatemala City, where we were likely to be surrounded by the many eyes of Interpol. Nobody was going to allow the Guatemalan Federales to gun us down in the street.

ME: What happened when you got there?

John McAfee: I didn't know what steps I'd have to go through when I got to Guatemala City. When I got there, I was taken into police custody by Interpol and put in jail, just before I was about to do a press conference where I planned to reveal some unpleasant truths about the corrupt nature of the Belizean government.

Simultaneously, that first evening, the Belizean prime minister, Dean Barrow, went on TV and said something to the effect of: "Mr. McAfee has been arrested in Guatemala. We have requested his immediate extradition. We will arrest him tomorrow, and he will be returned to us." That was his plan, but he didn't know I had Telesfero Guerra in my back pocket.

That first night, Telesfero brought this judge in who had the power to stay any movement of me from my current location until noon the following day. Meanwhile, they were to prepare an appeal to the courts, an appeal that the courts would have to accept, whereby Guatemala could ship me nowhere without my permission until my case was heard. But everything had to be done by noon; otherwise, Belize could simply collect me at the border.

ME: Why were you put in jail at all? Is this one of the times you faked illness?

JOHN MCAFEE: It was declared to the world that John McAfee was in jail in Guatemala for the horrific crime of entering the country without a passport stamp! In reality, I hadn't done anything anywhere that was worthy of anything more than a fifty-dollar fine. And yes. It's one of the two times I've done it, faked illness, in my life, and nobody will fall for it ever again, most likely. Simply put, it got to the point where I had to buy time until the court returned the appeal papers. That was going to be two hours at most, Telesfero explained. Before he left, he turned to me and said, "Do I need to give you further instructions?" "Nope. I'm good," I replied.

ME: So you faked a heart attack?

JOHN MCAFEE: Keep in mind that this policy works best when the eyes of the world are upon you. And the reason for that is that, in public view, the rules and common practices of medicine must be adhered to, all of which take time. This was my ace in the hole.

At a quarter to twelve, fifteen minutes before I technically could be collected, I was standing with the guards. Then I fell flat on my face and started performing convulsions, etc. Now, it didn't matter what they thought. They may well have thought I was faking, but it didn't matter. They had to go through the procedures because all of the world was watching. So, I knew they had to take me to the fucking hospital for appropriate examinations and tests. There were Federales at the hospital, but the doctors wouldn't let them in. Why? Television cameras.

ME: Where were the *VICE* people at this point?

JOHN MCAFEE: They weren't with me. But at some point, Rocco called me; I'd got hold of a mobile phone somehow. On that call, he didn't ask how I was bearing up in jail. No, he ranted and raved because the shirt I was wearing when I was arrested was a shirt of his that I had borrowed.

That is the God's honest truth—and Robert King will confirm that. Rocco completely unwound on this whole trip. He was not the man he said that he was. He just was not equipped to be following my ass around. He was naïve; he was always doing stupid things. And here he was, turning paranoid about a shirt and also his missing laptop. "That's my favorite shirt," he said. "I'm sorry," I said. "But right now, it's my *only* shirt!"

ME: Can I assume the doctors knew what was going on?

John McAfee: They weren't stupid. They had to have known. There were TV cameras everywhere and Federales outside. There are still pictures out there of me lying on my back with my head braced. When I'd been there for almost three hours to make absolutely sure, I sat up and said, "You know, I really do feel much better. I do not know what happened. I apologize. I am no longer a young man."

I was taken back to prison, by which point things started to become more comfortable as I'd found a way to get cash and was already bribing guards and wisecracking with the other prisoners. I wasn't just in a prison. I was in a Central American hole-in-the-ground prison. But within a few days, I had a mattress, internet connection, a television, two telephones, strawberries, McDonald's, and women. I was a minor celebrity in a Guatemalan prison—what a dubious claim to fame that was!

ME: What sense did you have as to what people in the US felt about this whole sequence of events? Did you care about your image?

John McAfee: I guess it was just what the press was saying, which was completely negative, not that I particularly cared. I was still an American, and to that extent, I knew what could and could not happen to me once I was returned there. Unlike Belize or Guatemala, there was no possibility of me being murdered in the street just because I was a bad man. So I didn't care. I was much more concerned with what people in Guatemala were thinking.

ME: And what were they thinking?

John McAfee: Well, during the three weeks for which I was detained prior to being returned to the US, all kinds of diplomats passed through to talk to me. Why? Because I had no problem whatsoever telling them whatever they wanted to know about their neighbor, Belize, with whom they were essentially engaged in a silent war over a meaningless strip of deserted land. I was a most valuable source of inside information to these people. That was one of the reasons they kept me so long.

They all sat and listened to my story intently. Of course, they all wanted names—which, of course, I had—and places—which I also had. I helped them with all that shit because, at that point, Belize had ceased to be my home. I owed it nothing. All the information I gave in no way harmed the Belizean people. But it damn sure harmed those in power, which is one of the reasons why I'm still on the run from these Belizean motherfuckers even now.

ME: What happened to Sam?

John McAfee: She was a loyal lady. She stayed by my side in Guatemala City the whole time I was detained, right up until the day that I was forcibly removed from detention and deported to the US. Of all the experiences that I've ever had, including love affairs, flying through canyons, and all these things, nothing has awed me more than the trip from the Guatemalan detention center to the airport in Guatemala City, where my plane was waiting to take me back.

ME: What, specifically, made you feel in awe?

John McAfee: I was in a military convoy. The entire boulevard, many, many miles of it, was totally devoid of other automobiles. On every street corner and rooftop were paramilitary forces with fully automatic weapons. There were spotters, scopes.... Why? Because, by the time they had let me out, the president of Guatemala himself sent his aides with a video camera so that I could tell him directly my story, including if I wished, anything juicy that I hadn't by that point told anyone else. By this point, Belize had to have figured out that I had spilled everything to their only real enemy, and because of that, there was every chance that Belize had mounted some kind of effort to stop me from returning to America alive.

ME: So the rooftop presence was there to protect you?

John McAfee: Yes. I heard later that Telesforo Guerra had said, "It is our highest possible priority that Mr. McAfee be delivered to that plane alive and intact." It was the safest I've ever felt. When I saw that level of security, in a poor country, I knew what it meant for them to mount an effort like that. They probably didn't even do it for their president. They sure as hell didn't want to be known for being the country where John McAfee got whacked. They just wanted me the fuck out of the country.

However, I get bored easily in cars. My mind started wandering. Typical of me, I remember thinking, *Ah, I wonder what I could do now and get away with that I could never get away with elsewhere.* And the answer was pretty much anything. I could have slapped the colonel sitting in front of me across the face if I'd felt like it. I could have punched the other guy on the back of the head, and nobody would have touched me. I could have pissed on the soldier sitting next to me with no fear of reprisal or consequences. Other than the physical limitations of the car environment, I felt like there was nothing I couldn't do! For a few minutes, I felt *omnipotent* and, simultaneously, a little childlike. When I was a kid, I dreamed of situations like that.

ELEVEN

BURIED

The latter stages of my conversations with Mr. McAfee were far less satisfactory than the early talks. It wasn't that he was getting bored; I don't think his reticence was related to our project at all. I just suspect, rightly or wrongly, that whatever net he always knew was out there with his name on it was starting to close in by the summer of 2020.

To that extent, it was no coincidence that our business relationship started getting strained. It was, after all, around this time that he first raised the insistence that he must only be paid in cryptocurrency. Previously, any minor disagreements he and I had regarding content, who to pitch the book to, whether coronavirus was real, etc., were resolved amicably and quickly forgotten. But the cryptocurrency payment insistence just wouldn't go away. In fact, the harder I pushed to resolve the matter or to look for viable alternatives—alternatives that would have been perfectly reasonable to anyone else I'd ever worked with—the more McAfee became angry and a little unpleasant.

There was a time when I might have taken this kind of reaction personally. Sometimes these things *are* personal. However, what I had to keep reminding myself was that, for all our conversations, all our pleasant message exchanges, and all his off-the-wall Twitter posts, his situation, in hiding, presumably somewhere in Europe, wasn't as pleasant a situation as mine was in my home. As much as we bonded, our lives were undeniably different and would never be the same. I started using his wife Janice as a means to indirectly encourage him to carry on, and, if possible, to reconsider the payment possibilities in the spirit of keeping the book alive. She tried. Janice always tries. But the decision as to how our project would ultimately be conceived was always in his hands.

ME: What did you think you were going back to as you sat on the plane?

John McAfee: I had my clothes and about five dollars in cash. Everything else had been taken from me when I left jail, which struck me as odd given that, apparently, I could have done anything I wanted when I was actually in jail. Nevertheless, I knew what I was going back to: America. Put me in America, and I'll always know what I'm doing. It will always be my home. Good God, I functioned well in a third-world dictatorship that was at war with me, so I had no worries about functioning at home.

I arrived in Miami with basically no money. The story of my arrival was bizarre. The plane didn't even go to the gate. It just sat there while emergency vehicles started driving along the runway. I thought, *Fuck me, what have I done to fall foul of Homeland Security now?* I had no idea what I'd done. We had serious officers coming up the stairs of the plane. Then the captain said, "Will Mr. McAfee please step forward...."

I raised my hand, got up, and started walking to the front while judging the faces ahead of me to figure out who was in charge. I identified a well-fed, nice-looking fella, and I walked straight up to him and said, "What have I done now, sir?" "Nothing at all," he replied, "but the North West terminal where you were supposed to arrive has two thousand news people there. We fear for your safety. We will be taking you to any place that you would like. And welcome home, sir."

ME: How do you even begin to start again after five years away?

John McAfee: I asked for them to take me to the nearest taxi stand. "Yes, sir," I was told by the officer, without any hesitation. They drove me there, and it was then that I realized they'd vacated an entire terminal at Miami International Airport. All there was at the end was a single yellow cab with a turban-wearing driver with both hands on the wheel, looking around and obviously wondering what the fuck was going on.

I got in the cab, told the driver to take me to South Beach, and thus began a new chapter in my life.

At one point, the cab driver turned to me and said, "Who are you, sir?" I looked back, thought for a second, and said, "I'm not sure anymore. But I don't have any money. If you take me to South Beach and are prepared to wait, I'll get you some."

When we got to this hotel, where everybody knew me and knew I was coming back, I got quite a reception. I know you might think I'm exaggerating this, but I had been top world news for over a month. To this extent, I knew I could count on the concierge for getting a room for a few nights without paying anything until I found my feet. I also got him to pay the taxi driver, who probably changed jobs or maybe even religion, with the tip I gave him on top of the fare.

ME: Janice is such a vital part of your life nowadays. Tell me how you two got together.

John McAfee: First, I contacted a guy called Francois Garcia from Venezuela, a promoter kind of dude. He had contacted me while I was in jail in Guatemala and persuaded me to start a website, to which I gave him certain rights to content, etc. I had his phone number, called him from the hotel, and said, "I need some money. Can you help?" "Sure, wait there." Twenty minutes later, this fat guy appeared with a paper bag. He sat down next to me and said, "You John McAfee?" "Yes, sir." He put the bag on the seat and just walked out of the hotel. There were $5,000, all of it in five-dollar bills.

Janice will confirm that, later that night, when I decided to go out for a decent cup of coffee and met her at my favorite place called the News Café, that all I had was five-dollar bills. On my way to the café, I had seen Janice and another white girl, both clearly hookers, walking towards me.

I didn't pay much attention, but as Janice passed me, I did notice what I considered to be a ten out of ten ass on her. I'm an ass man. That's a fact.

ME: Did she notice you looking?

John McAfee: As I turned, she turned too. She later told me that when she saw me first, her initial thought was, *Nah, that guy has no money*. She wasn't far wrong!

Anyway, I sat at the café and was enjoying my coffee when Janice appeared at my table. What she had done was gone past the hotel and chatted with the security guys as she often did. One had said to her, "Do you know who that man was that you passed earlier? John McAfee." "I've never heard of him," Janice replied. When he explained, Janice had come hotfooting it back to find me. Here she was at my table.

ME: Were you seeking female companionship?

John McAfee: For once in my life, no. I just wanted a good cup of coffee and a good night's sleep in an air-conditioned hotel room with a soft feather mattress. Nevertheless, the first thing that came out of Janice's mouth was, "Would you like your dick sucked?" "I am sorry, no. I do not want my dick sucked." "Can I have a cigarette, then?" I lit her a cigarette, and she and her friend sat down beside me.

"Are you girls out looking for old men to drug and roll? Because if you are, I'm not into that tonight," I told them. "Oh, we wouldn't bother using drugs," she said, which I thought was a particularly smart comeback. After a couple of hours of talking, I leaned over and said, "Can you get rid of your friend?'

Her friend evaporated. And as she did, I realized that I really did like this woman. We spent the night together. We didn't have sex. I didn't want sex. I'd had enough sex—even in a Guatemalan prison, where you can actually get some pretty nice chicks because all the pimps are incarcerated. Now, I just wanted someone to cuddle and to cuddle me.

We've been together ever since, even though, during that night while I slept, she was trying to figure out how to open the closet door, which creaked, so that she could steal my wallet! In the end, she didn't—and I'm glad. It would have ruined everything for me.

ME: How did your relationship progress from there?

John McAfee: There's something important I never told you. I have never told anyone this, and you'll know why when I do. I ask you to be open minded as we go through this next phase. You will not believe some of the situations I'm about to describe to you. When I was still with Jennifer, way back in 2005, when we were driving around the Southwest in my Hummer looking for potential airstrip sites, I was also burying stashes of valuable items and cash in various locations.

We buried items in places where nobody would ever find them. Unless you had GPS, you could never find the places. Over a period of a few months, I stashed away over a million dollars of valuable items: watches, gold, cash—all for a later occasion when I desperately needed it.

I'd just lost everything. And I mean everything: cars, money, my houses, etc. I owned nothing in the US other than an emergency stash of money that I'd started when I founded McAfee in 1987. That was where I got the money to pay Telesfero Guerra. So, when Janice and I first took a road trip in a car that I bought with cash, it was a long circuitous trip across the country, and the reason it was, was that I was stopping periodically to retrieve these buried items.

Janice kept asking me, "Why are we doing this?" Only later did I tell her. And I didn't tell her the full story because I never completely trusted her.

ME: You didn't trust the woman who is now your wife?

John McAfee: Yes, she's my wife. We actually got married twice. I'm not certain that the first time counted, but we are married. But—and this is where my story gets difficult to believe—Janice, for the first couple of years of our relationship while we were living in a house in Portland and, later, Tennessee, was conspiring against me in conjunction with other people.

ME: Who was she working with?

John McAfee: Initially, her pimp, who she was still in love with even though she was married to me. She was still seeing him, meeting with him in various hairdressers for black women, and strategizing with him by passing information to him about her location. He, in turn, was working with people who had connections with the Belizean government. Between them, they were trying to find a way to get me to return to Belize and get paid for it.

ME: This is mind-boggling. Did she ever actually harm you?

John McAfee: Several times. That's why, even now, when she brings me a cup of coffee, I always get her to drink some first. I'm in love with her, have lived with her for eight years, but I can't fully trust her. As I've told you, I trust nobody, not even myself. The first time she tried to poison me was back in 2013. She wasn't trying to kill me. The poison was only intended to incapacitate me to the extent that I could be collected. But, in the end, she couldn't go through with it.

At some other point, she hid her pimp and his gang in our attic in Tennessee. I came into the house and felt that something was wrong. In America, I carry a gun at all times: bedroom, bathroom, in the shower. I went into the bedroom, and I heard shuffling in the attic. Sometimes raccoons got in the attic, but this sounded bigger than a raccoon. So I just pulled my gun and went bam! bam! bam! through the ceiling. Security is worth more to me than the integrity of any house. Suddenly, there was a stampede, and the next day, her pimp called her and said, "Get them guns away from that ******!" It was only a year later that she told me that it was her pimp who was in our attic. It was for reasons like that that I always have a gun on my person at all times.

ME: Why were you living in Tennessee at all?

John McAfee: That was where John, my head of security, was at the time. He later turned on me and almost had me collected in Las Vegas. But that's a story we'll come back to later.

ME: Why were you with her when she was trying to sabotage you?

John McAfee: What I saw in Janice, and still see in her, was a kind of salvation for me. I made my life about saving her. I know you can't truly save anyone in this world, but I wanted to use the rest of my life to keep a door open for her that could be walked through into another world, should the one she was in become unpalatable.

ME: Did that become some sort of purpose for you? The Messiah complex again?

John McAfee: Yes, as much as I did love her and still do, it gave me something to do with my life. In some ways, I felt sorry for her because she had three kids who'd been taken away by social services because she was a working girl who was living with her pimp. The kids, who were from three different fathers, were living with Janice's father in California. After our trip across the country, we ended up in California, whereupon I insisted she visit her kids. She didn't want to, but I persuaded her anyway, even though I wasn't allowed in the house and was viewed with total skepticism by her father and her sisters. Understandably so, I suppose.

ME: Where did you go after California?

John McAfee: We made our way up to Portland, Oregon, because I wanted to see a friend, Chad Esley, who I'd met in Belize. Chad was a nice quiet guy, a cartoonist, and he'd come down to Belize to work on a comic book about my life but had ended up leaving, totally traumatized, having been thrust headfirst into my chaotic life.

ME: What happened to him in Belize? Did anyone not leave that country traumatized?

John McAfee: Chad was around when I was back in San Pedro, around the time when members of those two gangs I mentioned were threatening me. He was also there when I had the meeting with Eddie McKoy, the second most dangerous man in Belize.

ME: Eddie is interviewed in Nanette Burstein's film and seemed like a major component in all this. Yet, you have never once mentioned him until now. Why is that? The omission makes me very nervous—I've got to tell you.

JOHN MCAFEE: This is massively important. Remember I told you I was left a threatening note? Well, I did hire Rodwell Richards to find out who sent it, even though he was also working for the other side by that time, as most people like him often did. We found out that it was the White Lobster gang, and we managed to set up this meeting with two brothers, one of whom was gunned down a month after we met in Chetumal in Mexico.

ME: Do I need to know their names?

JOHN MCAFEE: Swan was their surname. So anyway, I was meeting with gang leaders who were after me, and my ace in the hole was always Rodwell Richards. I sat down with those boys, and Chad was there drawing cartoons in real time of all this random chaos that was unfolding. During this conversation, it transpired that Gaspar Vega, over in Orange Walk, was actually directing these Swan boys. They demanded the money. I refused. They said, "He'll send somebody else," to which I replied, "Then I'll deal with somebody else." They walked off. Meanwhile, Chad had drawn out this whole scene in cartoon form.

ME: I need to know about Eddie McKoy. I feel like you are avoiding this.

JOHN MCAFEE: Eddie was the somebody else, and I met him a few days later in the Sail Away Café that I'd bought Jennifer to run shortly after we moved down there. Eddie, as feared as he was, was a cripple. Years previously, he'd been captured by rival gang members, who sliced all the muscles in one of his legs. Even then, that bastard somehow managed to learn how to walk again, to the point where you might not have noticed if you weren't watching closely enough.

I found out about Eddie from someone, and they told me that he had taken an assignment to kill me. He had been paid $10,000 up front to kill me, with another $10,000 payable when I was dead. Eddie's nickname was Mac 10, because his modus operandi of whacking someone was to take all of his gang, the Mac 10s, and drive slowly past a house, shooting until there was nothing left. Everybody inside died. Babies, grandmothers—everybody inside died.

I called Rodwell Richards and said, "Eddie." And he said, "Yeah. You want me to take care of him?" Rodwell would have loved that assignment. Eddie was one of his major competitors. Eddie fascinated me. He made a lifetime business of whacking people. But that never happened, thankfully. But Eddie is still out there doing his thing. Nothing changes down in Belize.

ME: Did you ever pay Eddie to do anything? The film subtly led us to that implication.

John McAfee: No. The only person I ever paid in Belize was Rodwell Richards, and that was to threaten the drug dealers in Carmelita. Even after I returned to the US and was traveling around, being chased across the US with Janice, I still spoke to Rodwell once a week. It was he who told me that people in Belize were trying to engage someone in the US to pick me up. "They are going to try to kidnap you," he told me.

ME: Why did they want to kidnap you?

John McAfee: Among other things, they accused me of stealing sensitive records from government computers after I donated several expensive laptops to the Belizean government. That wasn't true. Every bit and byte were still intact. I just had a copy of them all. There's a difference! They still had it—so did I.

ME: We went in a circle there that I thought was leading somewhere. I still can't figure out if there was something I was meant to read into. In the meantime, what did you do when you got to Portland?

John McAfee: We leased an apartment on 20th Street; we got a couple of dogs, furnished it. It was very nice for a while, almost idyllic. At this point, I think there was some willingness on Janice's part to leave her pimp and side with me. But equally, looking at it from her perspective, I was this old white man who was wanted for murder in Belize. Was my character any better than that of her pimp's at that point? Arguably not.

But when something starts to feel comfortable, that's when I get wary. Nothing in my life has been idyllic for more than a few days. It's as if the universe detects something that's comfortable and decides to throw some chaos into the mix. That's the law of the universe. I start seeing more things and I start hearing more weird things that just don't add up.

ME: Such as?

John McAfee: The news that got me really thinking was when I heard that the Belizean soccer team was going to be playing in a tournament in Portland. Now, as far as I knew, Belize didn't even have a fucking professional soccer team. Any team they had was made of regular people like the local fireman or schoolteacher. And now, all of a sudden, they were coming to Portland? I'm not fond of fucking coincidences, and this information only confirmed what I'd heard from both Rodwell and a contact, Baltazar Garcia, inside the US embassy in Belize. I was on high fucking alert. And then I got a call from Baltazar, saying, "It's happening tonight."

ME: As in the collection attempt was about to happen?

John McAfee: Exactly. That night, Janice was looking out the bedroom window, and I was watching out the side window. When we leased the apartment, we had specifically chosen a corner lot that would give us a variety of views around the surrounding area.

Janice noticed that there was a man with a uniform on standing by a light pole. He looked like an electrical worker, but he was standing there with a flashlight, flashing this light on and off. In my experience, I knew he was signaling something to somebody else—probably to tell them we were in the building. I suddenly felt that we had to react, and fast.

ME: What did you do?

John McAfee: At one in the morning, I saw motorcycles, a black SUV, and a garbage truck coming down the street. I ran to Janice. All I had on was a pair of pants. I grabbed her and ran down to the basement, where the parking garage was. I wanted to hide in the dumpster. I always liked dumpsters because they were warm in cold weather. But Janice said, "I am not getting in the dumpster." Instead, we climbed up and hid under the back of one of the cars in this multi-level parking area. Within two minutes of us getting situated, the motion-detected lights went off. Then I heard a doorknob being turned, and then the lights went on again. And they stayed on for a solid hour thereafter. All we heard was slow shuffling in the garage. Up above, we heard footsteps and people running up and down stairs. At 3:30 a.m., the garbage truck came in. It was not the garbage day. They dumped the dumpster and then just sat there. Ten minutes later, we heard somebody shout, "Fuck!" They thought we'd be in the garbage dumpster. Janice saved my life.

ME: This is one of the most bizarre stories I have ever heard. Do you expect people to believe this?

John McAfee: I don't care if people believe it or not. This is the life I have lived. Janice and I were in a constant state of alert and fear. For basically four years we ran, while a cast of pursuers tried to track us down across America. They even tailed Janice's kids at one point, which was definitely a step too far.

ME: What happened after the Portland raid?

John McAfee: We found out later that the whole complex had been sold thirty days prior to the attack. And that it had been sold to an Armenian man who is now in jail for all kinds of things. He had formerly been a client of Belize's minister for national security. He had been in Belize regularly to party. That was the connection.

ME: Had he been contracted to collect you?

John McAfee: Yes. He had been paid by the Belizean government to try to collect me. But people continually misjudged how easy it always was for me to just walk away and leave everything I owned behind. We had furniture and all kinds of belongings, but we took a suitcase and the dogs, got in the truck, and left. We never went back to Portland or, in fact, the state of Oregon. We went on a run for almost a year thereafter. We were being continually chased. We never spent more than two nights in any town in America. We checked in late and left early. This was our life for a fucking year and more.

ME: Who, exactly, was chasing you?

John McAfee: We got chased into Arizona at one point because somebody shot at us on the highway with a high-powered rifle. We saw them in advance. As we were driving along the highway, we saw a Jeep parked in a field with a man lying over the hood. "Goddamn, that looks like a sniper," I said as I tried to pass the tractor trailer in front of us.

A shot was fired, and it hit the bumper of the tractor as I passed. The ricochet sounded like a flying saucer. We saw the metal flying. We got off the highway onto a back road. For an hour, we didn't see a single car coming the other way. Then we approached a single-lane bridge, beside which were parked two automobiles, each of them with four men inside. I slammed on the brakes, jumped out of the vehicle, and immediately looked behind me. I knew there'd be somebody coming. Nobody came from behind, so I basically barreled past the bridge while the vehicles moved aside to avoid a crash. They lost me. They always lost me.

ME: Was this still the Armenians after you?

John McAfee: Yes, and also, another former client of Belize's minister for national security, a very successful American businessman who I really cannot name, had, I believe, also been contracted to hunt me down. Also, I heard that the Sinaloa Cartel, given that it was also connected to the Belizean government, was another faction that was trying to collect me. At one point, they also had people watching Janice's kids. I had a friend in the cartel. Unfortunately, I can't name him either. I was speaking to him weekly. Sometimes I'd put him on speaker just to entertain Janice.

ME: How did you come to know someone in the Sinaloa Cartel?

John McAfee: I got to know him via his son. I did business with the son who was involved in a university in Mexico. I was helping them with cyber-security.

Anyway, when I found out that Janice's kids were being watched, I called this guy and said, "You have crossed the line. I have never harmed you and never spoke a bad word about you." "John," he said, "Do not worry. It's not me who is after you, but I know who is. I am your friend. I will always be your friend. In fact, you should come back to Belize. I have lawyers who can fix all this." Well, I just laughed. "Good God," I said, "Who do you think you're talking to?" But, after the call, the tail on Janice's kids mysteriously disappeared.

ME: Did you ever meet Janice's pimp in person?

John McAfee: No. I only ever talked to him on the phone one time, and that was when we were in Portland in 2013, while she was initially trying to get away from him. Anyway, he called, and he and Janice were yelling at each other. "Give me the phone," I said to Janice. She handed me the phone with her pimp still on the other end. "This is John," I said. "You send Janice back now, or I'm going to send up a gang to cut you to pieces," he said. "Well, if you really want to do that, please inform everyone to bring their own body bag because I am sick of buying body bags." "Don't you get gangster with me!" he said. "Please," I told him, "I'm not threatening anyone. But please just have some common courtesy." He hung up the phone. That's the only time I ever talked to him. I do not scare easily!

ME: So, did this all continue until you left the country in 2019?

JOHN MCAFEE: On and off. We had periods where things calmed down. The first year and a half was the worst. We even went to the FBI to report what was happening. They did nothing. We became reasonably friendly with an undercover cop who worked for the FBI in Colorado. His name doesn't matter. But he had some stories to tell himself. He had been physically threatened by members of an Islamic terrorist cell that the FBI had infiltrated down on the southern border somewhere. He told me that members of this cell pursued him when they realized that the FBI had discovered them. He also told me that somebody had tried to shoot him through his office window at some point. "Nobody believes what's happening to you," he told me. "But I do." My story was his story.

ME: Could you even trust the FBI at this point?

JOHN MCAFEE: We got to become reasonably good friends. He was a low level agent, not a manager or anything. I went into his office one day and said, "I know for sure that someone will approach you one day asking if you'll whack me. How much is that going to be worth to you? One million dollars? Two? Ten? What if they kidnap your daughter and start sending her fingers to you in the mail or pictures of her minus an ear?"

"I know what you're saying," he said. "But let me be frank with you: you always come into my office with a gun. So if I choose to shoot you in the head, the biggest problem I would have would be vacating the office for a couple of days while they cleaned your blood off the walls. Do you understand the power of this position?" In that moment, while I appreciated being told this information, I couldn't also help acknowledging the power that government agencies had. Basically this guy was saying that he could shoot me, or perhaps anyone, at any time, with no consequences. It was so revealing.

Anyway, when things cooled off a little, we went to live with my head security advisor near Lexington in Tennessee. Mike had worked for some serious mob bosses in Chicago and came highly recommended when I hired him to look after property of mine in Rodeo, New Mexico a few years earlier. But when I left the US to go to Belize, he didn't go with me because I didn't think I'd need him. However, he remained very loyal in my absence and I "activated" him again when I went on the run. It was he who got cash to me in Guatemala for example. It made total sense that he should be my bodyguard now that we were back in the US. He was one of the few people I thought I could trust—and I use the word trust very loosely. At that point I barely trusted myself.

For about six months, Janice and I were not comfortable living anywhere other than in Mike's house—more of a nicely done double wide on a huge piece of property, which was three hours from Memphis. He and his wife vacated their master bedroom and gave it to Janice and me. Because Mike didn't work for anyone other than me at the time, he was always home. They had two mastiff guard dogs, and the property had expansive views across the surrounding countryside. If anyone came into the neighborhood, we'd know about it almost immediately. This was real rural country where they basically lived by their own set of rules. They still made white lightning moonshine in illegal stills; if a stranger crossed the blurred boundary that separated rural Tennessee from urban civilization appeared, someone would stop them and say, "Why are you here? Who are you looking for?" It was perfect for us. Other than for the first month when a few curious strangers passed through, we had no harassment

ME: What were you doing for money at that time? Did you work on any business ventures?

John McAfee: Well, I didn't need to do much because we were living with Mike and his wife, eating their food and contributing to their basic expenses. I was working, but only to the point that I was accepting speaking engagements at conferences on the subject of cyber-security. I was in great demand and could charge $25,000 or even $50,000 for each appearance.

After a period of time, it becomes uncomfortable living with another couple, especially when you are John McAfee. So Janice and I bought our own house, fifty miles from Mike's place, in a small town called Lexington. We were close enough that Mike could come and sleep the occasional night as security.

However, now that we were living in our own house, things changed and that's when Janice's dynamic and her relationship with her pimp became a problem. There were various intrusions, including when Janice's pimp was in the attic. One of the houses we had to sell because it leaked so much on account of all the shotgun blasts I'd fired through the walls at people I thought were prowling around outside. I wasn't trying to kill anybody. I was just hoping that the blast would be close enough of a warning to any intruder that it would scare them off. Eventually, we had to stuff these holes with towels and clothing to keep the place watertight. None of that stuff bothered me, however. I only ever had one goal: staying alive.

ME: Why did Mike not stop this if he was a security guard?

JOHN MCAFEE: Mike, sadly, turned on us in the end. Although he kept his financial problems a secret from me, he ended up having to file for bankruptcy and was so desperate for money that he accepted a bribe to *not* be at DEF CON in Vegas to protect me on one occasion when I was a guest speaker. As I said before, an attempt was made to pick me up. I evaded that attempt too.

ME: At what point was Janice totally on your side?

JOHN MCAFEE: You are making some very broad assumptions, my friend. I'm not even sure she is now. Please, God! But seriously, I *think* she is now, but only because she has followed my ass for so long that she's now in more or less the same trouble as I'm in. They want to arrest Janice just because of her proximity to me.

While Janice has serious street smarts—ten years on the meanest streets of America as a prostitute will give you those—she has no experience in how to avoid the clenches of corruption in government and law enforcement agencies. For me, that's my fucking specialty. If I have to have a specialty at all, it's fucking with governments and law enforcement agencies and using my speed to simply sneak away or make myself invisible. Without me, life would be very difficult for Janice. So, 75 percent of her is on my side. And right now, those are percentage odds I'll happily take.

ME: For what reason did you leave Tennessee for North Carolina?

John McAfee: Latterly, our house in Tennessee, had been on a lake. Being on a lake is fine, but when you love boats like I do, you realize that a lake is just a fucking lake. After an hour, you've been everywhere. But the ocean...that's infinite. So we bought a house on the sound side of Hatteras Island, which is surrounded by some of the most interesting, roughest waters anywhere in the world. I then bought a small boat and also a larger boat and thank God that I did.

ME: Why was the grand jury convened in the first place?

John McAfee: At the end of 2018, I heard about the convening from two separate sources, two weeks in advance of when it was meant to happen. On behalf of the IRS, myself, Janice, and four of our compatriots were being charged with unspecified tax fraud charges. Grand juries are only convened for felonies. Felonies mean serious jail time. However, I knew this was coming. I had not paid tax for ten years.

ME: Why not?

John McAfee: I'd just had enough. I'd paid $50 million in income tax over the years. I thought that was plenty. I hadn't paid tax since I went to

Belize, but, technically, as an American citizen, even if you're not living in the country, using the services, and driving on the roads, you still have to file and pay 30 percent of your income to the United States. The only two countries in the world that enforce that rule are the United States and Eritrea! How fucking bizarre is that? Anyway, I just said, "I'm sorry. This is insane. I'm not doing this anymore." For a while, nothing happened.

ME: What changed?

John McAfee: In 2017, after my presidential run, I started going onto the international stage to talk about cryptocurrency. I was in Stockholm, London, Barcelona; I showed up wherever anyone would have me, and I said the same thing: "Cryptocurrency can free us from the imprisonment that existing currency has put us in." "What business is it of our governments to know what we earn?" I also said many times.

I then explained how the dollar and pound, etc., are controlled; the supply can be influenced, which, in turn, can devalue people's hard-earned money and how everything is monitored through the central banks. I then explained how, in America, income tax is, in fact, unconstitutional anyway. It was only ever created to fund the war effort in 1913, but that edict, like many others, was never extinguished after the original need for it ceased to exist.

ME: You were basically encouraging people not to pay taxes.

John McAfee: I was telling people that I thought taxes were illegal, and if they also felt that they were illegal and/or unjust, they should just stop paying too. Not just that, I was showing them how to do it without getting caught.

Now that hit a nerve, as I knew it would. Here's the thing: I'm not here just to mouth off. No, I am here to goad and to prod my enemy. I like doing that, just like the Apache Indians had something called "Counting coup," where they knew they could kill their enemy but preferred to poke them repeatedly and run away. Basically, I was annoying the shit out of my enemy. But all of this goading finally tipped the balance.

ME: So did you get any warning that they were looking at you?

John McAfee: I got fair warning because the IRS and SEC started subpoenaing records from companies that I was connected with in the States. That was a sign that they were watching me. Most men in my situation would have simply shut the fuck up. Instead, I started talking louder.

Grand juries are intentionally top secret so that people can't run. But I'm John McAfee. You can't keep a secret from me, especially if you're my government. I don't just listen to one source and take it as gospel, though. I got the information verified by another source. And based on that information, we knew we had until a certain date to leave the country.

ME: If you hadn't fled, would someone have literally turned up at your door?

John McAfee: Absolutely, they would have swooped in and collected me in my home at 6 a.m.—with particular emphasis on swoop—and I'd have probably been thrown in jail for the rest of my life. I wouldn't be able to talk to you. I wouldn't be able to talk to the press. I might be in hiding now, but I get more exposure than ever. Plus, I am still prodding that hornet's nest as often as possible.

Since I've been on the run, I have posted publicly on Twitter things like: "The SEC is a festering pustule on the face of America." I don't know how you goad them any more blatantly than that. It's my job to do it because, more than anything, I want the government to show its true face. We can all put on a face, including our governments, but only when it's poked hard enough and it responds hard enough does it show the world what it really is. And that's what I'm trying to do with the US government. I want the world to see that what's happening to me could also be happening to them and, in twenty years' time, could be happening to everybody if I don't at least continue my fight.

ME: Was there a specific reason you left America and sailed straight to the Bahamas?

JOHN MCAFEE: I went to the Bahamas simply because they had no income tax, and therefore, I couldn't be extradited for a crime that doesn't exist in the country where I was residing or visiting. International law prevents that.

I figured we'd stay three to six months, but we only lasted three. Given there was no legal way to collect me in the Bahamas; I knew that they could only go down the illegal route. But the illegal route takes time, especially when you're dealing with me, the slipperiest motherfucker on the planet. I knew they couldn't slip up, couldn't get caught, and that it would take time to organize and plan any sort of collection.

Sure enough, after three months, I started getting word that the CIA, on behalf of the State Department, on behalf of the FBI, on behalf of the IRS, was planning to do something.

ME: How does this information get to you?

JOHN MCAFEE: Keep in mind, when I started McAfee back in the '80s, my primary enemy was the hacking community. I admired most of them—truly, I did. These were bright young kids. And later, when we got into the era of groups like Anonymous, some of these people even had a strong fucking message: Freedom. "Privacy. Just give us fucking privacy."

Over the years, especially after I left McAfee, I became something of a prime target. Just imagine how much of a badge of honor "I hacked McAfee" would have been for someone. So, in turn, I got very adept at protecting myself, and, in doing that, I realized that disinformation and deception are far more powerful than any barrier you can erect to try to stall your enemy, because, given the history of warfare, we know all too well every barrier is eventually overcome. Disinformation, on the other hand, though? That's powerful stuff. Making your enemy believe you're on the other side of the hill? Making the enemy believe that you're dead? Well, that's powerful shit.

ME: Are you a hero to the hacking community?

John McAfee: Over the years, I certainly became very friendly with the hacking community. In fact, I was invited to speak at DEF CON in Vegas in 2014. Incidentally, somebody tried to collect me that night because they knew I'd be there. But now, the hacking community are collectively my closest friends to the extent that there is nothing involving my name that might impact me, that does not reach me almost instantaneously.

Bear in mind, there are hundreds of thousands of dedicated hackers in the world, and I doubt there is a single one who does not consider me to be their brother or their patriot and, in many cases, even their leader. For those of them that are reading this book, I hope this relationship continues because they have saved my life more times than I can count.

ME: Were Anonymous involved when you were on the run in Belize?

John McAfee: They were, but that was an instance when the hacking community wasn't especially helpful, ironically. I had started my blog to tell my side of the story while Anonymous, that loose group of who knows who, had shut down every internet department in Belize as well as all communications to and from the country. I'm sure they probably thought they were helping me, but I was in hiding above the Chinese warehouse in Belize City and needed access to my blog in order to keep my story alive online.

I ended up having to send someone into Guatemala to make a phone call to someone in Boston to say, "Please, God, stop!" A few hours later, everything was restored. It's scary what power these hackers have, and they really are my ears to the ground nowadays.

ME: Is the information always reliable?

John McAfee: Generally, it is. But anytime I have a suspicion that something is off, I can put out a specific message that says, "Can someone please verify this specific area of interest," and I'll get hundreds of responses from which I can, by process of elimination, work out what is happening. It wasn't like I knew these people's real identities or had a phone number I could call, but that's fine. One way or another, the information always seemed to reach me.

ME: So it was the hacking community that tipped you off about the raid that planned in the Bahamas?

John McAfee: Yes, that's where the information came from, and I acted on it. Paul Rolle, the police commissioner of the Bahamas, in conjunction with the long chain of command from the IRS, was trying to have me arrested as an undesirable. That way, they wouldn't need to extradite me because there would be no law or court involved. Had their plan worked, I would simply have been expelled back to the US. That's how they wanted to bring me in. But they failed, and I ended up embarrassing Paul Rolle in the process by revealing sensitive and embarrassing information relating to payments he received from a CIA agent gone rogue. I received information that the collection was about to happen, but just before we shoved off with the yacht fueled and ready, I called the Bahamian newspaper and gave them Rolle's private bank account details and the details of all the transactions that had gone into it and from whom. It was a parting shot from me as if to say, "You motherfucker. You mess with me, and I'll show you what I can do."

The next day, as we were on the way to Cuba, a news story appeared in the Bahamas, saying, "Paul Rolle sues John McAfee for defamation of character." By that time it was too late. I'd left that Bahamas. I just thought, *Feel free to sue me as much as you'd like.*

ME: Why did you go to Cuba next?

John McAfee: By this time, it was very clear to me that all bets were off in terms of the US ever attempting to collect me legally. The events in the Bahamas had illustrated that, by fair means or foul, they were determined to bring me in as soon as possible. I was embarrassing them. It couldn't continue. Meanwhile, they now knew I wasn't going to go anywhere where I could be picked up legally. So, we arrived in Cuba. It was a strange country and very nice.

After a month or so, Janice and I were called in and asked to turn up at a military installation, which, in reality, looked more like a Greyhound Bus shelter. Nevertheless, we went in and sat down on easy chairs. We weren't prisoners in a cell, nor were we in a room with a friendly environment like an American boardroom.

Someone said, "The US government has unofficially asked us to return you to America, in return for certain concessions." At that time, American warships were just off the coast of Cuba. We could see them. America did this from time to time, as if to say to Cuba, "Listen, we can't touch you, but we are still the power. So you better toe the goddamn line." They then said they were disinclined to make us leave but that it would assist them greatly if we left within seventy-two hours.

Eventually, they would have had no option but to get rid of me. Me being harbored by Cuba, a communist dictatorship, was only going to heap further embarrassment on the US. As the day approached, the Cuban authorities called around regularly, saying, "Now, Mr. McAfee, you are *sure* you'll have left within forty-one hours, yes?" "If I have to swim to Haiti, I'll be out of here," I told them.

But again, I knew how serious all this was. If the US was actually appealing to Cuba, a country that it had beaten back into the Stone Age with sanctions over the years, well, that told its own story. But I didn't know how serious it all was until four days later at sea when we arrived in the Dominican Republic and saw military *soldiers*—not just the police—lining the dock. The rest, my friend, you know. Everything that I did in the Dominican Republic was focused on one thing: how to not get sent back to America.

ME: Are people from Belize trying to track you down as of right now in 2020?

John McAfee: Well, I have since lost my ears and eyes down there. I have had no information from anyone in Belize for a while. Baltazar Garcia doesn't answer his phone. The very thought of Rodwell Richards just scares me nowadays more than anything else. Any other friends I had down there, like Eddie Ancona, were leaned on. Others were imprisoned; others were killed I truly believe. There is just no recourse to law in a country like Belize.

ME: So is it a case of out of sight, out of mind regarding Belize for you now?

John McAfee: Yes. I haven't really said anything about Belize for a while, and I'd imagine they like that.

ME: Are you taking drugs again now that you're in hiding? You mentioned that when you need them, you're going to take them.

John McAfee: I don't really take the drugs that normal people take. Granted, I do a bit of cocaine, marijuana and methamphetamine, but I'm much more interested in the Chinese chemical research industry. This isn't shit to kill plants; these are chemicals for modifying people's behavior. Why do the Chinese want to do that? Well, with two billion people, they've got more behavioral problems than anyone. And the research isn't just aimed at their population; it is also geared towards warfare.

Twenty years ago, I established relationships directly with some of these manufacturers—to the extent that, whenever my name comes up in China, you wouldn't believe how much people like me. We were swamped when Janice and I went to talk at a conference in Beijing in 2016. I was bemused. I had no clue how anyone knew how the fuck I was. I got out of a taxi at the Great Wall and this guy ran up to me shouting, "John McAfee! John McAfee!". I couldn't believe it.

Anyway, I digress. These Chinese chemicals have been an important part of my life because they are a very potent part of my life. So yes, I take them and yes they modify my behavior. You tell me how you'd like to feel or act, and I can come up with a concoction to make that happen.

ME: I have to ask you something that you may not like. It has been suggested by many that you are just paranoid, that you have always been paranoid. I can see why. What do you say to that?

John McAfee: I've heard that before, and it's just a preposterous suggestion. Indeed, if anyone is paying attention, pretty much everything I've ever been alarmed about to the extent that I've felt the need to warn other people has happened. People said I was exaggerating the need for internet security back in 1989. People said I was just being paranoid. Who was right?

I've warned people about privacy and government intrusion for years. Who was right? I knew what was happening in Belize when the government was conspiring to frame me. Who was right? I am not paranoid, my friend. I just happen, as I've told you several times, to have a good feel for impending doom. And if I can warn people when I sense something coming that could potentially affect us all, nobody can stop me from saying so.

And as I've also said, I am now an old man who has to rely on my wife Janice to be my eyes and ears. I can't always trust my perception, mainly because I still think like a thirty-year-old. I remember when I was at an event in London a few years ago. People were crowding around me—young, insanely hot women still throw themselves at me, God knows why. In my mind, I think these women actually want me. At no point do I think, "Why would a twenty-year-old goddess want anything to do with a seventy-five-year-old man with bad knees?" At no point do I think, "This doesn't feel right. Who has sent you?"

However, Janice does. She knows every fucking move any woman on the planet can possibly pull. She just stands there, observing. On that trip to London, this chick came up to me, put her room key in my hand, and whispered in my ear. Janice removed the key from my pocket, politely handed it back, and said, "He won't be needing that." I'd been thinking with my ego, my dick. Janice was thinking, "This girl might look like an angel, but really she's a she-devil with a fucking icepick." To that extent, Janice and I are the perfect couple. We are truly in this together until the very end.

ME: How does this position make you feel?

John McAfee: Well, let me just say that being in hiding and on the run are two completely different feelings. When you're on the run—as we were for five months—you're out there saying "Here I am people. Come and get me if you think you can." As you're saying that, you know that they're not going to be able to do that without spending time and resources, which in turn allows you to move to the next place. But when you're in hiding, which we have been since we were sent back to London and then covered our tracks completely, nobody knows where you are and it is going to take time to collect you, planning, resources and greasing of palms. In hiding, I am relaxed. And here we are.

EPILOGUE

If somebody had asked me, "Do you think John McAfee will ever get captured?" I would have probably said, "No." I'd reached a point where, extremely naïvely, I really believed that this seventy-something man that I'd been talking to for months was invincible. After all, his track record wasn't half bad. One way or another, by fair means or foul, McAfee had somehow managed to avoid total calamity on many, many occasions.

However, his luck ran out in October of 2020, and I had mixed feelings when I heard about his arrest in Spain, when he was apparently attempting to board a flight to Istanbul while traveling on his British passport. In the months after we stopped talking about book material, our contact drifted as COVID-19 took hold.

When he went on Twitter claiming that the pandemic was a hoax while deaths mounted around the world, I winced uncomfortably. When I read the bizarre story (which turned out to be fake) about him supposedly being arrested in Norway while wearing a thong mask, I laughed. Both of these incidents were pure McAfee: controversial, contrary, provocative, and more than a bit playful.

I reached a point in 2020 where, as much as I had all the material from our conversations, I also didn't have an obvious way to publish it once he jumped ship, all because of the issues with being paid in cryptocurrency. I had two choices. The first was to put it all down to experience, save the files and move on. Nothing about doing that felt good. Much time and energy had been invested in the process. Not just that, but the content felt like it might be compelling.

The other possibility was to publish the material. But to do that, I simply did not feel comfortable proceeding without his blessing. As much as we had disagreed, and the end of our talks had been a little frosty, I felt that to publish these intimate conversations without his approval would amount to something of a betrayal. I did not feel comfortable about betraying this man. It wasn't that I cared about repercussions. He was in hiding, clearly had no money, and almost certainly had more pressing problems to contend with than shutting down a book about his life. I didn't want to betray him because, despite his many faults and the multiple aspects of his life I just didn't understand or endorse, a part of me still cared about not only the man, but also what he thought about me.

So I reached out to him via our usual Skype messenger method.

"Hi, John. I'm thinking about writing a book using our conversations. What do you think?"

"OK," came the reply.

Afterward, we formalized it by email. I wanted him to confirm that he was absolutely fine with my using our conversations in a book. He confirmed by return that he was.

Now, some people might say, "Who could possibly care about a man wanted for murder, a serial adulterer, and a self-confessed king of misinformation?" And on some levels, they'd be right. However, to me, there was an element to McAfee that made me consider that maybe he has led the kind of chaotic life that many of us wish we, too, could lead.

Let me be clear. When I say that, I'm not referring to the aspects of his life that were illegal/morally questionable. I'm referring simply to the ability he has always had to simply submit to the chaos of the universe and to see where that took him—and to do it all with absolutely no regrets. Speaking personally, that's something I really admired about John McAfee: his ability to try on a new persona like a pair of new clothes, wear it, see if it works, and then tear the whole outfit off and start all over again when it doesn't. That, to me, is the essence of living.

Now, granted, I totally understand that to be able to live like that, a person needs to be free of commitments and have plenty of money to burn. If I tried it, I'd probably be living on the street in a matter of days. Let's be honest, few have the kind of latitude to live the kind of life John McAfee has. But maybe, just maybe, there's a lesson to be learned in the way McAfee has lived, not to mention the manner in which he is willing to turn the mirror back on himself.

People have asked me if I think I got the truth out of John via our many discussions. I can't say with 100 percent certainty that everything McAfee told me in the months for which we spoke is true. I'm not even certain if he knows what's true at this point. What I do know is that everything he said was said in a way that made me believe that this was a man who wanted, finally, to give the world a fleeting glimpse of what made him the man he is. I doubt it's the full picture. What picture ever is? But I felt that, given his age and situation, it was the closest we may ever get. That might be my ego talking there, but time will tell, I suppose.

I was in touch with Janice in March of 2021. As I often did, I passed on my best wishes to John, who by that time had been in a Barcelona jail for eight months. The details of this book were about to appear online. Again, I wanted to let John know so that he wouldn't hear it from someone else.

"I have relayed your messages to John. He told me to let you know that your book has his full support. We both look forward to reading it when it's out."

It felt like a satisfactory position, and I hoped our next contact would be when the book came out and/or John was released from prison. But the story wasn't over....

POSTCRIPT

On June 23, 2021 I was sitting in my kitchen, scanning through news articles on my cell phone, while intermittently flipping between my Twitter feed and responding to direct messages. Halfway down the feed was an article saying that the court in Spain had approved McAfee's extradition from Spain to the US to face tax fraud charges. I felt an instant knot forming in my stomach. I knew what this meant. Or at least I thought I knew.

An hour or two later, I saw another Tweet by a news editor who was quoting Reuters and saying that John McAfee had been found dead in his jail cell in Spain.

I fucking lost it.

I walked upstairs to my office, the office from where I conducted every conversation with the man back in 2019 and 2020 and around which his laugh often reverberated. I sat at the top of the stairs, desperately trying to process this gut-wrenching and completely unexpected information. My visceral reaction took even me by surprise. I threw shit. I kicked out at the wall. I actually *cried*—and I'm a grown man of fifty-one years of age who barely cried at my own father's funeral. My wife, hearing the commotion, actually came and comforted me. She, too, albeit vicariously, had lived through months in the world of John McAfee.

The days that followed were a blur of sadness offset by doubt and confusion. On one hand I was desperately sad that it appeared that prison had broken the McAfee spirit that had fought so hard to keep him alive: faked heart attacks, faked strokes, flight from Belize, pursuit across America, and pursuit around the world. Throughout it all, McAfee's life force had been strong. At the age of seventy-five, as he was at the time of his death, McAfee's desire to keep living, albeit under duress, seemed to be undiminished. Yet, despite all of that, the man lay dead in a federal facility in Catalonia, having reportedly been found hanging in his cell with some kind of a note in his pocket that the Spanish authorities seemed quite willing to take as a suicide note. To me, it didn't read like an intelligent man like John McAfee's final farewell to the world.

Inevitably, conspiracy theories exploded, literally within minutes of his death. Had he committed suicide? Had he been killed to ensure his silence about information he once claimed to have about US government figures? Was he dead at all?

In the days after John's death, I was contacted for comment by a number of outlets that wanted my view, based on my relationship with him, on whether suicide was likely.

As much as I wanted to get ahead of the story by cutting through some of the hype, at that time I was still reeling with shock and was unable to process what had happened well enough to articulate in the way that I wanted. All I could do was say that, based on the will to live that he had always expressed in our talks, it was a surprise to me that John McAfee would have taken his own life. Furthermore, when I heard that he'd given no indication to Janice that suicide was his frame of mind when they last spoke the previous morning, it all seemed even more implausible given how close I knew those two were.

However, I couldn't ignore the flipside to this argument, and that was the nature and tone of John's tweets in recent months. While he often suggested that he was relatively happy in prison, all things being equal, and that the relationships he had with younger inmates, many of whom considered him to be a father figure, were gratifying, there were other occasions where his tweets suggested that eight months of incarceration, with no visits and little access to regular legal recourse, were starting to take their toll.

When I considered all of this, I must admit that I did find myself thinking, *Maybe John just gave up?* even though it soon became clear that, although the judgement had gone against him regarding the *concept* of extradition, the practicality of his situation was that it would be a year plus until he'd be moved anywhere, in addition to there being multiple other legal plans already in place. Basically, this judgement wasn't unexpected. John knew it was coming; it was more a matter of when and what the options were thereafter.

The suggestion that his death had been the result of foul play was no easier to assess in the days immediately afterwards, not in any way helped by the fact that McAfee had previously tweeted to say that, if he was ever found dead like Jeffrey Epstein had been, it wouldn't be a suicide. In a separate tweet at a different time he had also suggested that if anything was ever to happen to him, there would be an automatic release of the damning information he claimed to have.

This theory of a "dead man's switch" (DMS) was certainly the most popular with the media in the short term. Indeed, every media outlet I spoke to wanted to know whether I thought that the existence of a DMS was even possible and, given my insider knowledge gleaned during our conversations, whether I knew anything of this information he had referenced.

The reality of the matter is that I was no more informed than anybody else. John had, of course, mentioned government corruption on a conceptual level in our talks many times and, as you'll now know, he did mention a rogue CIA agent who attempted to have him collected, whose name I know but omitted in the text even though this was information that John himself had already made public at the time of his departure from the Bahamas when the agent apparently tried to bribe a Bahamian police official. Other than that, that's all I knew. But knowing McAfee as I did, I also knew that nothing is ever for sure or clear.

An hour or so after his death, a Q appeared on a blank background on his Instagram page before later being removed. Now, I do know for sure that John rarely, if ever, accessed that account. To my understanding, the only social media that he actively engaged in was Twitter.

To that end, the Instagram post was a mystery—a mystery that became a lot more mysterious when hackers/tech types established that the code behind the Q image was somehow connected to an Ethereum wallet with some kind of link to the Whackd cryptocurrency coin that echoed the tattoo John had on his arm and the terminology he used to describe the act of being murdered in a couple of his tweets.

At that point, honestly, I just let the wild conspiracy theories go. I didn't have either the information or the willingness to dig any deeper into it all in the days immediately after his death. I was still thinking too much about John McAfee's life to get too weighed down in examining some of the possibilities surrounding his death. That, depending on what transpires down the line, is something for another day. Regardless, people kept asking. And I kept saying, "I don't know."

I was more interested in the details about where John had been laying low, especially given that this location was where he'd been throughout our talks.

As it turned out, the location, a place called Daurada Park Hotel, an hour south of Barcelona, wasn't especially glamorous. However, when I saw the images online of this previously Russian owned beach hotel that had reputedly been closed in 2018 because the owner had mounted an industrial laser on the roof, I immediately recognized the coastal backdrop as the same view I'd seen behind him when we talked on our many Skype calls.

Apparently, the place was being run as a bitcoin mining operation—perfectly legal in Spain, by the way—with a whole host of complex and extremely expensive computer technology installed in an underground garage from where the actual mining took place. It was suggested that the owner had installed the laser on the roof as a means of explaining the property's abnormal energy consumption given how much electricity it requires to mine bitcoin.

On some levels, this location made sense. Maybe whoever was running the operation was the person John referenced in the bizarre foreword he sent me early in the process? That seemed feasible, as did the existence of a bitcoin operation generally. Cryptocurrency was, after all, John's world.

What made much less sense was that he was in Spain at all, and not being especially careful about what he posted on social media while he was. Indeed, it was amateur local sleuths who discovered his location from online images and the presence of unique Spanish products in them.

To me, for someone who had been so careful and secretive, it made no sense that he was in a country like Spain from where he could be reached and extradited, living in plain sight in a relatively touristy beachside area. Had he been in Serbia or Montenegro or somewhere similar (good luck finding anyone there, far less extraditing them) that would have made much more sense.

But it was what it was. The Daurada Park Hotel was where it had all gone down, and in my few attempts to speak to anyone on the ground in Spain, all I could establish was that the place was now closed down and heavily guarded.

Above and beyond all the mystery surrounding his death, and in addition to the fact that I was in touch on a daily basis with his US lawyer, members of his immediate family and his close friends, and was being asked to talk about the man in some kind of official capacity to the media, I found myself torn in the aftermath of John McAfee's death.

On one hand, I didn't want anyone to think that I was using John's death as an opportunity to simply sell a book. Indeed, as I've explained, the book was actually finished (apart from this part of it) long before John's demise. As far as I was concerned, the book was going to come out later in the year, John was going to endorse it and promote it as he said he would, and that would be it. Hopefully, his legal issues would have been resolved, and he and I might have met in person some day and had a laugh about it all.

But when he died, everything changed. Suddenly I was left with this man's life story as told to me—a life story that I knew beyond doubt that he wanted told no matter what.

So I had no choice. I went out there in the media and talked. And as time passed and the rawness eased somewhat, I got better at saying what

I wanted to say. The bottom line is that John McAfee had so much to say to the world—especially a world that's in as much turmoil as this one is right now. As far as I was concerned, when John died, the responsibility to let his words be heard became mine. The man treated me well. The least I could do was uphold his legacy in return by encouraging people, at a time when his name was on everyone's lips, to make themselves aware of this book we'd worked on together.

That was my motivation in June 2021, and it will continue to be long after the book is published. Will there be other books about John McAfee? Probably. I for one would be interested to read them. But this one, particularly given the circumstances by which it was conceived and the style in which it is delivered, I hope will be considered fitting as the last will and testament it often felt like he was relating to me.

ACKNOWLEDGMENTS

To my family, I can only thank you for tolerating the slightly obsessed person I became during all of this. You always stand by me—and accept that "this," what I do, is just part of me. I take none of that for granted.

I want to thank Jacob Hoye for his support throughout this unusual process. I think even he would agree that it took a bit of persuading on my part to convince him that this format would work! But we got there. Everyone else at Post Hill Press for the sterling effort in the background to make this happen and get the book out—I thank you.

And finally, to Mr. John David McAfee, for engaging in the first place, endorsing my ability, and being open to me making this book what it now is. I can never thank you in person beyond the letter I sent you in prison that was later returned unopened by the Spanish postal service. But I can thank you here. So long, Gringo. It was nice knowing you.

ABOUT THE AUTHOR

Mark Eglinton is a Scottish author and co-writer. His recent books include *Blindsided*, with former Australian rugby captain and stroke survivor Michael Lynagh, which was shortlisted for International Autobiography of the Year 2016; *Heavy Duty: Days and Nights in Judas Priest* with musician K.K Downing, one of the top ten music books of 2018 according to *Rolling Stone*; and *Reboot: My Life, My Time* with football legend Michael Owen, shortlisted for Autobiography of the Year 2020 by the *Daily Telegraph*. Among other endeavors, he's a former professional golf caddie and has written about his experiences for *Golf* magazine and *Golf Digest*.